GAINED HORIZONS

Other titles of interest from St. Augustine's Press

James V. Schall, *The Regensburg Lecture*

James V. Schall, s.j., *The Sum Total of Human Happiness*

Nalin Ranasinghe, *Socrates in the Underworld: On Plato's* Gorgias

Marion Montgomery, *Making: The Proper Habit of Our Being*

Marion Montgomery, *Romancing Reality:* Homo Viator *and the Scandal Called Beauty*

Marion Montgomery, *With Walker Percy at the Tupperware Party*

Peter Augustine Lawler, *Homeless and at Home in America*

Josef Pieper, *In Tune with the World: A Theory of Festivity*

Josef Pieper, *Happiness and Contemplation*

Josef Pieper, *The Silence of Goethe*

C.S. Lewis, *The Latin Letters of C.S. Lewis*

Rémi Brague, *Eccentric Culture: A Theory of Western Civilization*

René Girard, *A Theater of Envy: William Shakespeare*

Edward Feser: *The Last Superstition: A Refutation of the New Atheism*

Roger Scruton, *On Hunting*

Roger Scruton, *An Intelligent Person's Guide to Modern Culture*

Roger Scruton, *The Meaning of Conservatism*

Peter Kreeft, *The Philosophy of Jesus*

Peter Kreeft, *Jesus-Shock*

Jacques Maritain, *Natural Law: Reflections on Theory and Practice*

Leszek Kolakowski, *My Correct Views on Everything*

John Paul II, *The John Paul II LifeGuide*™

St. Augustine, *The St. Augustine LifeGuide*™

Michael Davis, *Wonderlust: Ruminations on Liberal Education*

John Poinsot, *Tractatus de Signis: The Semiotic of John Poinsot*

Thomas Aquinas, *Commentary on Aristotle's Nicomachean Ethics*

Thomas Aquinas, *Commentary on Aristotle's De Anima*

Thomas Aquinas, *Commentary on Aristotle's Metaphysics*

Thomas Aquinas, *Commentary on Aristotle's On Interpretation*

Thomas Aquinas, *Commentary on Aristotle's Posterior Analytics*

Thomas Aquinas, *Commentary on Aristotle's Physics*

Thomas Aquinas, *Disputed Questions on Virtue*

Thomas Aquinas, *Commentary on the Epistle to the Hebrews*

Thomas Aquinas, *Commentary on St. Paul's Epistles to Timothy, Titus, and Philemon*

John of St. Thomas, *Introduction to the Summa Theologiae of Thomas Aquinas.* Translated by Ralph McInerny

St. Augustine, *On Order [De Ordine]*

GAINED HORIZONS

Regensburg and the Enlargement of Reason

Edited by Bainard Cowan

ST. AUGUSTINE'S PRESS
South Bend, Indiana
2011

Manufactured in the United States of America.

1 2 3 4 5   17 16 15 14 13 12 11

Library of Congress Cataloging in Publication Data
Gained horizons: Regensburg and the enlargement of reason /
edited by Bainard Cowan.
p. cm.
Earlier versions of all the essays were given at a colloquium at
Assumption College, Sept. 21–22, 2007.
Includes bibliographical references.
ISBN-13: 978-1-58731-325-7 (pbk.: alk. paper)
ISBN-10: 1-58731-325-1 (pbk.: alk. paper) 1. Faith and reason –
Christianity. 2. Benedict XVI, Pope, 1927–. 3. Catholic Church – Doctrines.
I. Cowan, Bainard.
BT50.G35 2010   230'.2 – dc22

∞ The paper used in this publication meets the minimum requirements of
the American National Standard for Information Sciences – Permanence of
Paper for Printed Materials, ANSI Z39.48-1984.

ST. AUGUSTINE'S PRESS
www.staugustine.net

Contents

Acknowledgments

Earlier versions of all the essays except Nalin Ranasinghe's were given at the colloquium "The Regensburg Moment: Benedict XVI and the Rediscovery of Reason," at Assumption College, September 21–22, 2007.

For their indispensable sponsorship and support I thank especially those at Assumption College who helped make that colloquium possible: President Francesco Cesareo; crucial support from Vice President Dennis Gallagher, A.A., and Director of the Ecumenical Institute Gavin Colvert; administrative help from Vice President David Marker (ret.) and Dean Eloise Knowlton; Janet Lambert, Laura Lawrence, Mary Willis, Carmella Murphy, Nancy Cain, and Andria Hoffman, all of whom spent extra hours helping to realize the colloquium; and Dean Mary Lou Anderson and colleagues Nalin Ranasinghe and Daniel Mahoney for encouragement and much needed advice. My gratitude goes also to the Intercollegiate Studies Institute and to Mark Henrie for its contribution to the support of the colloquium. Thanks to Bruce Fingerhut of St. Augustine's Press, whose confident guidance in this project sped its transition from colloquium to book. My greatest debt however is to my spouse, Christine Cowan, who encouraged, debated, edited, suffered, and sustained me through this entire project.

Introduction

Bainard Cowan

The abrogations of reason in our time are not only plenty but endemic. A small but important example will suffice. In grading hundreds of college essays each year, I find students always writing that "Wordsworth feels," "Aquinas feels," "Shakespeare feels" rather than any of these writers "arguing," "claiming," "thinking," "believing," "averring," or any other activity of the mind. This repetition is more than mere carelessness. It is an abrogation of reason that has crept into the very structure of our thinking and responding. It is sentimentalism, the belief that (or the acting as though) in human affairs feeling is all that matters. Further, it insists that any inquiry into right and wrong is a betrayal of feeling. How can we possibly judge someone's actions unless we walk that mile or two in their shoes and feel what they feel? As a corollary, it holds that the existence of powerful irrational forces in the human makeup negates the existence of reason or, if not its existence, its authority to sit in judgment of those forces and attempt to govern them.

Sentimentalism has powerful allies in its attack on reason in the modern world. Particularly when the scientific method is enlisted to tackle a complex human problem, it confers a sense of continuing a hallowed quest for the pure self-founding of reason, for which one is only too glad to confine one's inquiries to the narrow ground of "objectivity" (which too often turns out to be merely consensual non-contradiction). This *faux* reason (or perhaps incomplete reason) then installs proceduralism as ruler over human judgment. How often do we see logic touted as the savior of a situation, when clearly the assumptions the logic works on have not been examined at all?

Caution about the mind's tendency to deceive itself is certainly warranted, but when the bar is raised so high that reason is taken out of the grasp of the nonspecialist and claimed as the prerogative of the scientist, mathematician, or logician, it is only a brief step until those specialists themselves come under suspicion for hijacking reason for their own purposes. When the scientist in his white lab coat and the engineer with his pocket protector became figures of ridicule some few years back, that point had arrived. No longer was anyone—ordinary person or Ph.D.—seen as harmless, much less beneficial, in using reason. The suspicion of all things (all people and all motives) became the ultra-sophisticated hallmark of postmodernism, with its value-free pervasive belief that the games of power to seduce and control us are infinite.

Only one small, baleful step from postmodern cynicism, however (perhaps even embedded in it), is the *worship* of power. The cynic who drops out is replaced by the cynic who takes charge. It is hardly a step at all to conclude, with technocrats and market analysts, that since power is the only factor that makes significant differences in our lives, power is truly the only thing that matters.

In their many forms, these assumptions about our world have become so pervasive as to be almost unnoticeable. We don't pay much attention to them unless an adamant teacher or analyst makes us take note, but our attention span is short. Since these attitudes, predilections, assumptions, and actions seem to have no harmful impact on our economy or on our personal liberties and because we have learned to be myopic, to see only as far as the individual, we fail to notice that the long-standing institutions that enabled the Western world to undergo the modern revolution are now crumbling. More and more, the church, the university, and ultimately the state are playing their roles in name only: they have been hollowed out from within so that actions are performed as mere convention and nothing within them is concerned with the central qualities, ontological and metaphysical, that make human life worth living and worth understanding.

Against this background, Pope Benedict XVI's lecture "Faith, Reason, and the University" to the Evangelical and Catholic theology faculties of the University of Regensburg on September 12, 2006, would hardly seem able to make a difference. After all, if anyone thinking, speaking, or writing is able to express only subjective opinion, then this must be doubly so for religious leaders, who, the heirs of Marxism and Freudianism assure us, have built their rhetorical castles on the shifting sands of illusory feelings masquerading as traditions. Further, as if to corroborate that dismissive assessment, the Pope included a passage that offended many Muslim spokesmen, when he could just as easily have left it out—proof, it would seem to them, that he must have been unable to sublimate those pervasive urges of survival and territoriality.

Yet Benedict's honest straightforwardness had its effect, a better effect than repeating the usual platitudes could have had. The open letters written to the pope by Islamic religious leaders in response to his talk have led to meetings and now the establishment of a Catholic-Islamic Forum and other signs that the Muslim world has brought the question of its own aggression into focus for itself.

The pope's call to Muslims to consider their positions anew was only an indirect example prefacing his main argument, however. To his German university audience and implicitly to all Christians, Benedict issued an unmistakable call to respect and approach anew the dual heritage of Western culture, its "rapprochement between Biblical faith and Greek inquiry" (#19).[1] Not merely a historical coincidence but an "intrinsic necessity" (#19), their collaboration was, he declared, "of decisive importance ... from the standpoint ... of world history" (#29). This message stands in bold relief against the present climate of opinion in which our civilization has lost respect for both heritages: the Greek sense of form and order that gave birth to Homer and the great tragedies, out of which sprang Socrates and the entire unique endeavor of Greek philosophy to clarify the roots and ends of human existence; and the Hebraic experience of a creator God who, while not revealing himself except in his creation, called them personally, encapsulated as Benedict avers in "the mysterious name of God, revealed from the burning bush" (#20).

The recovery to which Benedict is calling his listeners addresses a threefold problem. First, the robust Greek undertaking of knowing the world and ourselves through reason has been degraded and undermined in our time. Second, the even more robust understanding of faith worked out in the Hebrew Bible, which includes a call to community and to openness to God's burning love, has diminished to a thin stream of hoping against hope. Finally, to speak of an "inner rapprochement" (#29) between the two inheritances could not run more counter to what is widely taken for granted, that to begin to speak of faith is to check reason at the door, that faith flies in the face of even a crippled reason. Yet Benedict links Abraham and

---

[1] Throughout this volume, quotations of "Faith, Reason, and the University" are taken from the text printed as Appendix I of James V. Schall's *The Regensburg Lecture* (South Bend: St. Augustine's, 2007), 130–48. References are to the numbered paragraphs in this edition.

Socrates in a common "process" (#21) transcending the bondage to myth in the human mind. This rapprochement, this process, requires a refurbishing and deepening of our understanding of both reason and faith.

One of the most concrete ways to submit faith to the review of reason is dialogue between or among religions. It is interesting that, in quoting from a dialogue with an educated Persian by the fourteenth-century emperor Manuel Paleologus, the Regensburg lecture succeeded in bringing back into currency the very form of encounter to which that medieval dialogue testifies: the disputation on propositions of religious truth. Jacob Neusner has referred to this form, in examples such as Judah Halevi's imaginary narrative "Kuzari," in praising the pope for a contentiousness equal to his own. "Such debates," observes Neusner, "attested to the common faith of both parties in the integrity of reason and in the facticity of shared Scriptures."[2]

The form of the Regensburg lecture itself, however, recalls the *Schwellendialog* or dialogue-on-the-threshold that the great Russian literary scholar Mikhail Bakhtin saw as a thematic pattern in the *Apology* and the *Phaedo*, "the summing up of a man on the threshold...a tendency to create extraordinary situations, which cleanse the world of all automatism and objectivization and force the person involved to reveal the deepest layers of his personality and thought."[3] James V. Schall, S. J., who has already devoted an entire book to exploring its implications, compares Benedict's lecture to Pericles' Funeral Oration, Plato's Apology, Lincoln's Gettysburg address, and Dostoevsky's Pushkin Monument speech, all exemplary dialogues on the threshold. Of course Benedict was not standing at the edge of the grave or the battlefield, nor is his speech an interchange with other speakers. Nonetheless his extraordinary openness and frankness, the way in which he revealed himself and placed his belief on the line, draws on the threshold dialogue tradition that, as Bakhtin attests, finds its roots deep in the human soul.

What is this threshold that Benedict stands on with us so precariously perched beside him? It is not some new danger to which the substance of his lecture alerts us, for the loss of the love of truth has been a long process in Europe and America. What warrants us to speak of the "Regensburg Moment" as a significant turning point, a threshold, is that it presents a

---

[2] Jacob Neusner, "My Argument with the Pope," *Jerusalem Post*, online ed., 29 May 2007, www.jpost.com/servlet/Satellite?cid=1180450948925&-pagename=JPost%2FJPArticle%2FPrinter.

[3] Mikhail Bakhtin, *Problems of Dostoevsky's Poetics*, trans. R. W. Rotsel (Ann Arbor: Ardis, 1973), 91.

possibility of waking up from the dominating forces that alienate and make impossible the question of truth: sentimentalism, mechanical determinism, subjectivism, all those things that have removed the right and proper use of reason from our lives. Intellectually, spiritually, metaphysically, the Regensburg Moment is an opening to the soul, allowing it to see this damage, even amputation, to which we have become numb.

Benedict's message—that the conception of God as reasonable is a central Christian and Western tenet—has enormous repercussions for Catholics, Christians, and Westerners alike. Because Christianity takes seriously, and not merely sentimentally, the notion that God is also love, reason and love (*ratio* and *caritas*) cannot be separated from each other. To separate reason from love is to handicap love, to cripple it and prevent its efficaciousness. Accordingly, Benedict says in his address that "Christian worship...is worship in harmony with the eternal Word *and with our reason*" (#28, emphasis added). Our love, praise, and gratitude find their most vivid and fulfilling expressions in rites and rituals that channel those effusions into forms that bring out their depths on the one hand and that connect us with the whole community of believers on the other.

Metaphysical and Baroque art and poetry especially understood that reason requires going to extremes precisely because it is to be equated with love, in a cosmos in which God himself could maintain the constancy of the good only by subjecting himself to death. In a poem such as "Good Friday, 1613. Riding Westward," Donne employs the Ptolemaic system even as it is being steadily discredited by new science, attached to it as he is here and in other poems for its implicit first-principle metaphysics. Nonetheless, he transforms it in his argument in this poem to the function of an analogy. Reason exists in both the subject (the movement of the spheres) and the form of the poem (an argument about what he should be paying attention to: seeing God die in an act of humility and all-encompassing love). Further, the argument leads him to understand paradox after paradox ("a Sun by rising set/And by that setting endless day beget"; 'hands which span the Poles,/And tune all spheares at once, pierc'd with those holes"; "that endless height which is/Zenith to us, and to'our Antipodes,/ Humbled below us").

After experiencing the Crucifixion through imagination and meditation, the speaker concludes his rational examination of Christ's death with an outpouring of love. He prays to be corrected, to have his rusts and deformities burnt off, that the perfect image of God in him might be restored (a mirror no longer dark) so he would perfectly reflect God's love back and, the crown of all, be known fully—rationally and emotionally—by God.

In this final image of correction becoming perfection, which the modern world would see as masochistic (why would anyone wish to be punished unless he were emotionally and psychologically troubled or abused?), we see the metaphysical comprehension of the intimate communion of reason and love: reason (and only reason) leads the speaker to the foot of the Cross, the font of complete love, where he is convinced by his argument to seek that love and offer his own (incomplete) love in return in the hopes that he will be lifted up to a higher comprehension and a fuller sacrifice.

A number of Metaphysical poems, Donne's in particular, dramatize the interaction of reason and love as they fulfill and supplement each other in human endeavors. The extremes to which the poems take both reason and love (each work follows the argument to the furthest extent and portrays love as overflowing and excessive) attempt to capture the divine in human terms, bringing the transcendent and the immanent together in a poetic experience. The contrary movement, expressed in the Cartesian meditations from that same time period, reduce reason to what is supposedly scientific but result in the West excluding reason from its renewing and purifying source in love. Reason could affirm only what it knew in and of itself, cut off from love entirely in the little bare room of Descartes' meditation.

Here in these two seventeenth-century images, the baroque Cross of Donne and the solitary thinker of Descartes, are embodied the choice that Benedict presents. Reason conjoined with love in the Cross opens the soul to community, dialogue, and health; reason reduced to logic and deprived of any connections to the world closes the soul and makes it rely on itself, to its detriment and self-imposed disease.

Benedict seeks to restore the dialogue and interchange between reason and love, and not incidentally between theology and the other human sciences, by rejuvenating the arguments for the close relation of Christian theology to reason. Elsewhere he has readily acknowledged that "there exist *pathologies in religion* that are extremely dangerous" and require the response of reason (the best reason that we can come up with): "Religion must continually allow itself to be purified and structured by reason; and this was the view of the Church Fathers, too."[4] However, he also concludes that "there are also *pathologies of reason*...a hubris of reason that is no

---

[4] Joseph Ratzinger, "That Which Holds the World Together: The Pre-political Moral Foundations of a Free State," in Jürgen Habermas and Joseph Ratzinger, *The Dialectics of Secularization: On Reason and Religion*, ed.Florian Schuller, trans. Brian McNeil, C. R.V. (San Francisco: Ignatius, 2006), 77. Subsequent references are given in parentheses in the text.

less dangerous" (77–78). Reason as a human faculty must exist within the same limits as the human soul to be healthy. Pathologies arise when reason becomes solipsistic and obsessed. "Reason, too, must be warned to keep within its proper limits, and it must learn a willingness to listen to the great religious traditions of mankind. If it cuts itself completely adrift and rejects this willingness to learn this relatedness, reason becomes destructive" (78). Its proper stance is attentive, patiently listening, and setting about restoring a good order, as inclusively as possible, to the contentious claims of the world. Hence there is "a necessary relatedness between reason and faith and between reason and religion, which are called to purify and help one another" (78).

Characteristic of Benedict's style are a lucidity and concision that allow him to condense huge and lengthy developments into a few clear sentences that shed new light on a complex phenomenon. Although the Regensburg lecture is a particularly concise expression of Benedict's insights on the centrality of the dialogue of reason and faith to Western civilization, it is hardly a new theme, for he insisted on it repeatedly in his years as Cardinal Ratzinger. One of his central points emerges in a discussion of the impact of the encyclical *Fides et Ratio* issued by his predecessor, John Paul II, when he remarked that it is "a duty of humanity to protect man from the dictatorship of what is accidental and to restore to him his dignity, which consists precisely in the fact that no human institution can ultimately dominate him, because he is open to the truth."[5] For Benedict the very survival of freedom and human rights depends on this openness, which can be maintained only by an affirmation of the efficacy of human reason. The Regensburg lecture continues this central theme that Benedict has recurred to in many of his public speeches.

A brief summary of the lecture is perhaps in order before we go on to consider the common purpose of the essays in this book. In "Faith, Reason, and the University" (which was chosen as Address of the Year by the renowned School of General Rhetoric of the University of Tübingen), Benedict emphasizes that an essential principle of Christianity is the claim that "not to act in accordance with reason is contrary to God's nature" (#14). That God's transcendence does not preclude the openness of divine precepts to examination by reason is shown by the early Christian "rapprochement between Biblical faith and Greek philosophical inquiry" (#29). The quest for reason to overcome the crisis of myth and tradition exists as

---

[5] Joseph Cardinal Ratzinger, *Truth and Tolerance: Christian Belief and World Religions*, trans. Henry Taylor (San Francisco: Ignatius, 2004), 191.

a dynamic in both lines and is "accompanied by a kind of enlightenment" in each (#21). In the Late Middle Ages the church reaffirmed that "between God and us ... there exists a real analogy" (#27) against arguments that reason is not a reliable way to know God's will, even though God's "unlikeness remains infinitely greater than likeness" (#27).

Benedict goes on to outline the "dehellenization of Christianity" (#31) throughout the modern age as a long process occurring in three stages. The first of these, the Reformation with its emphasis on *sola scriptura*, was followed by the liberal theology of the nineteenth century, based on "the modern self-limitation of reason" as expressed by Kant and "radicalized by the impact of the natural sciences" (#40). Here Benedict explores the irony that though those sciences testify to "the rational structure of matter" (#59), the excusive reliance on the prestige of the scientific method reduces reason to the mathematical and empirical. In this view "questions about our origin and destiny ... have no place within the purview" of reason and must "be relegated to the realm of the subjective" (#48). Particularly, "ethics and religion lose their power to create a community and become a completely personal matter" (#49).

In the third and most contemporary stage of de-Hellenization, reason itself comes to be considered as merely a Western cultural construction, an arbitrary predilection. In opposition, Benedict maintains that "the world's profoundly religious cultures see this exclusion of the divine from the universality of reason as an attack on their most profound convictions" (#58). He concludes with a call for the recovery of "courage to engage the whole breadth of reason" (#62) even as we continue to look outward for "partners in the dialogue of cultures," for "to rediscover it [the breadth of reason] constantly is the great task of the university" (#63).

Clearly the last words of his lecture point to the university as the place where it is most urgent to reestablish the dialogue of reason with faith, religion, and love, its broader, sustaining sources. In his discussion of the Regensburg lecture, Schall reminds us that the university lecture itself is a manifestation of the Christian belief in reason, for the principles of "free inquiry, clarity of statement, conditions of logic, and comprehension of the whole" were standards imposed by the Medieval university, the exemplum of theology and reason working in unison.[6] It is through the training of the university that we know how to act habitually with reason. How many universities today are aware of this awesome responsibility?

---

[6] Schall, 39.

To return to that threshold on which Benedict and we stand (or teeter), we find it has several coordinates. One is the university lecture hall, whose utterances will confirm the good or poor health of reason in the society at large. The second exists in the threshold between faiths (including the faith of no faith), a potential or actual war zone unless genuine dialogue can illumine differences and renew belief with reason. The third threshold is that between human and divine reason; it calls human reason away from a narcissistic concern with self-consistency and reaches always for a broader conception of reason, a dynamic conception that is indeed restless until it is one with divine love. The need for a dialogue between reason and faith is the crucial issue in all these spaces.

These three areas then are our common human concern; they will form the outlines of inquiry and discussion for years to come. Although it is not possible to explore in this short space these areas of contemporary life in which the interplay of reason and faith are crucial, we begin the work the pope set for us. Several of the most distinguished and most stimulating figures now writing on the public scene have come together in *Gained Horizons* to focus on the challenges and hopes of reason. The first several essays focus especially on the confrontation of reason with voluntarism, both at home and abroad, and the dangers that arise when the primacy of will forces reason into a merely supporting role.

Jean Bethke Elshtain combines several of the thresholds in her essay. She begins by finding in the conception of a God who is approachable by reason the root of the Western conception of limited monarchy, in which rulers are subjected to law, even and especially to the laws that they themselves have made. This, she argues, is the essence of the openness of divine reason. God's nature, which is love, shows itself in following the laws he himself has created, thus making the laws into precepts that human beings can know and rely upon. Augustine and Thomas Aquinas held that God's power is "ordained power," Elshtain notes, and that means that that power is knowable. Islam's tradition, unlike the Christian, does not see God as the *Logos* but remains largely a religion of will. Elshtain makes the connection clear between a religion of will and a politics of force on the one hand and a religion of *logos* and a politics of freedom on the other. She goes on to call for a more honest dialogue of Christianity with Islam that will openly air differences and criticisms, for only then will it be possible to hold insights in common. For this to happen, however, the West must regain belief in the principles that made it great. Those who speak for the West, she argues, must know confidently the difference between tolerance and capitulation. They must not lose sight of the true and the good, and for this they must be educated better.

Peter Augustine Lawler expands on the threshold of human and divine reason, in particular as it plays out in America. For him, America, like the modern world, is both de-Hellenized and de-Christianized, but both operations are carried out in quest of freedom for the willful human person made in God's image. He criticizes our belief that "we can know everything but the being who can know," which debilitates our reason. Seeing Pope Benedict as articulating a science adequate to the achievement of the American Founders and thus a science it is urgent for us to recover, he hopes thereby to counter or reform American public opinion, which tends both to deny reason in the name of freedom and to rigidify reason in the name of a democratic science available to all. The cure for what he calls "American nominalism," the tendency to regard reason as arbitrary, is "more science, not less," specifically the science of theology.

Human and divine reason is also Marc Guerra's subject as he emphasizes the mutual nurture of reason and faith, seeing it operating at the heart of the Western tradition. As he shows, this dialectic was in operation even before Christianity in the Greek dispute between philosophy and tradition, resulting in an original de-Hellenization or demythologization that was hardly to be regretted. The process was incapable of resolution, however, until Christianity's announcement of a kingdom "not of this world." With this proclamation, Guerra insists, Christianity turned its back on the "political theology" that Carl Schmitt and other critics have claimed is at the core of all religion.

Nalin Ranasinghe warns us of the difficulties if we ignore the threshold. In explicating the meaning of the "Regensburg Moment," he argues that the pope's lecture, which highlights the fact that reason as developed in the Greek tradition is an essential aspect of Christianity, actually makes possible a turn in the self-understanding of the West. This comes at a crucial time, he remarks, for clearly a technological market culture cannot be a civilization unless it acquires a renewed regard for truth and the good. If we do not seize this moment, he insists, the alternative is grim, for we are headed into decline and violent clashes without understanding our path in or out.

Bruce Fingerhut's essay focuses on the threshold between faiths. He remarks that the voluntarism whose danger is the subject of much of the Regensburg lecture was the very source of the violent response to it. The greater danger, however, is in the voluntarism that Benedict shows to have been long active in Western thought. The emphasis on will over reason, he notes, produces a "weakened god" that must inevitably leave its subjects defenseless in attack. Such a watered-down religion inevitably means that a dialogue between faiths would be ineffectual, if not harmful.

The next two essays are concerned especially with ways of conceiving a broader scope of reason: in literature or Augustinian philosophy. They take the threshold of divine reason and examine how it plays out in specific authors. Glenn Arbery develops the description of man imprisoned in theory as the vision of Dostoevsky's *Crime and Punishment*, seeing the modern "self-limitation of reason" imaged in Raskolnikov's claustrophobic garret in St. Petersburg. In this setting, Raskolnikov's theoretical relation to the world turns a pawnbroker woman into an abstract proposition and ultimately into the object of his violence. For Benedict, the reason the natural world is rational "is a real question," requiring investigation by the sciences of philosophy and theology. For Arbery, literature too plays a special role in this urgent investigation. Great literature restores the multidimensionality of the lived world around us, a world whose image is flattened in the news and the stream of ordinary discourse with which we always encounter that world. It is a flat world, too, in its representation in philosophy, as it serves only to instantiate general principles. A masterpiece like *Crime and Punishment* restores the analogical dimension to our experience, making it available to our knowing in a way that philosophy not only is incapable of doing alone but actually depends on literature for achieving.

The task of reclaiming an understanding of reason that is broader than the application of logic could not be more urgent, for any culture will surely die if it is without openness to transcendence through the power of reflection that is innate in the human mind. Michael McShane contributes to this reclamation project through a close examination of Augustine's understanding of Christianity in the *Confessions*, finding in the African doctor's meditations a discovery that God is beyond logic, that in many ways to think of him is to embrace contradictions, but that he is nonetheless the transcendental source of reason.

The final two essays address the threshold of the university, its discourse, and the very act of teaching. The location of Benedict's speech in the distinguished German university, with its two theological faculties, provides a thematic setting, for his lecture examines the nature of the university, its commitment to reason, the place of theology in the university, the grounding of faith in reason, and the need for a robust conception of reason to underlie any dialogue among faiths, between faith and culture, and between faith and science. Although arising naturally out of the setting, these matters both provoke our imagination and discomfit our souls R. R. Reno observes that the last two popes have both been committed to the defense of the life of reason, alerting their audiences to the dangers posed by the "undesirability of truth" in the contemporary university. Because we have lost a mooring to truth, we "have lost the confidence that the disciplines ... can help us understand how we can live our lives." Paradoxically, however, Reno shows, the loss of orientation toward truth has made professors in the humanities "moralistic" and "strident," more certain of their arguments than ever, since arguments are all they have to rely on. Hence reason has been, literally, de-moralized. Calling for a recommitment to the adventure of reason, Reno writes in praise of a discredited virtue, docility, without which there is no quest for truth but only sophistic struggles of empowerment.

Mary Mumbach relates the courage Benedict demonstrated in delivering his lecture to Socrates' courage in Athens. Both men provide analogues to what she reminds us is the courage required of the college teacher on a daily basis, though this is a courage that current practice and the higher educational system militate against in multiple ways. Mumbach's meditation is a torch piercing that systematic night, encouraging professors to profess, that is, witness to, reason in the works they study.

In his Address to Catholic Educators during his visit to the United States, Benedict acknowledged the difficulty of the struggle of education at the same time that he exhorted his audience to renew it: "God's revelation offers every generation the opportunity to discover the ultimate truth about its own life and the goal of history. This task is never easy ....Set against personal struggles, moral confusion and fragmentation of knowledge, the noble goals of scholarship and education, founded on the unity of truth and in service of the person and the community, become an especially powerful instrument of hope." We offer the essays in this volume in support of that difficult but vital task.

Regensburg and Reason: Benedict XVI Against Absolute Will

Jean Bethke Elshtain

In his anti-religion tract *The Future of an Illusion*, Sigmund Freud permitted himself a rare moment of something akin to optimism. One day, he opined, the "still, small voice of reason" would triumph over all illusory, wish-fulfilling belief systems. Religion, specifically, would go the way of the dinosaurs by fading into extinction as one of those childish things we put away when we become securely adult. Freud's hope has not come to pass, of course, and the irony is that one of the most eloquent defenders of reason on the world stage today is the head of the church Freud considered a potent foe, the Roman Catholic. With Pope Benedict XVI's Regensburg Address, reason fairly rings from the roof-tops: it is no "still, small voice" we hear but, instead, a clarion call to a reasoned faith. Where Freud had reckoned all religious belief systems irrational illusions, Benedict parses matters quite differently by distinguishing between faiths that call upon human beings to approach God through reason and love and, by contrast, those that stress submission to a voluntarist God who is the apogee not of reason but, rather, of will. At the same time, Benedict distinguishes the reason of which he speaks that is central to the faith he espouses from narrower forms of rationalism such as positivism that have over the years equated themselves to reason *tout court* and thereby downgraded forms of knowing beyond the ken of one limited epistemology: a tall order for a concise address.

Given the occasion and his own limitation of his material, Benedict could not treat the issue of voluntarism and will within the Western theological tradition in any detail, though he did note some family resemblances between those tendencies within Christianity and the currents Benedict finds in Islam that downgrade God's reason in favor of God's will. At the same time, these currents of thought in both religions diminish human free will while extolling human submission to God's implacable will. Given the brouhaha and outbursts of violence in the streets in some Muslim-majority countries following the distorted and even hysterical accounts of what Benedict actually said, Benedict's criticism of developments in Western culture went largely unnoticed.

My first task will be to assay briefly competing understandings of God's being or nature in Christian theology, beginning with Benedict's discussion of the voluntarist strains in Western theology. In the Regensburg Address, Benedict notes the following: "In all honesty, one must observe that in the late Middle Ages we find trends in theology which would sunder this synthesis between the Greek spirit and the Christian spirit. In contrast with the so-called intellectualism of Augustine and Thomas, there arose with Duns Scotus a voluntarism, which, in its later developments, led to the claim that we can only know God's *voluntas ordinata*. Beyond this is the realm of God's freedom, in virtue of which he could have done the opposite of everything he has actually done" (#25). Benedict adds that this "gives rise to positions which…might even lead to the image of a capricious God, who is not even bound to truth and goodness" (#26). And this sort of capricious God brings God closer to the views in the Koran that the Byzantine emperor Manuel II Paleologus had criticized, as quoted by Benedict, in the passage that invited the subsequent uproar.

This is worth exploring a bit further. The central question and puzzlement is this: if God's power is absolute and immutable, is God in any way bound, or is he free to undo what he has already done, overturn the laws of nature perhaps, or even bring creation arbitrarily to an end? No, said Augustine and Thomas, or the synthesis of the two that had emerged and culminated by the late thirteenth century. In this view God's power is bound (*potestas ordinata*) rather than unbound (*potestas absoluta*). Let's clarify this distinction. God's absolute power refers to the sum total of the possibilities available to God before he acts, limited only by contradiction. That is, God cannot act in direct contradiction to himself.

Ordained power refers to what God does and the way God does it, which is reliable and regulated. Both notions of power presuppose that God is sovereign in the sense that he enjoys a plenitude of power not available to, or attainable by, mutable earthly powers of any kind. God's reason, including wisdom refracted through the Thomistic system, is fully compatible with Christian revelation. Divine reason enjoys a priority over divine will. We have access to God not only via revelation but via reason. Our access to God through reason, superadded to the mediation of the Second Person of the Trinity, draws God closer to humanity. This interpretation spurs one strand of concern: if we are so close to God or, rather, if God is so accessible to us, what happens to God's omnipotence, his awesome power that stuns us into wondering and worshipful silence?

This debate flares up from the eleventh century on. Consider the views of the eleventh-century thinker, Peter Damiani, whose topic is the divine omnipotence. Argues Damiani, God "has no need of any creature and is nudged by no necessity to create, drew out of that nothing into existence this natural world of ours, establishing its order, imposing upon it its customary laws. Incapable in his omnipotence and in his eternal present of suffering any diminution or restriction of his creative power, that natural order he could well replace, those laws at any moment change," for God "can undo the past—so act, that is, that an actual historical event...should not have occurred."[1]

Damiani's God is the possessor of an absolute power whose "essence...is to be self-sufficient perfection," with creation an arbitrary act. By contrast, the Thomistic God, lifted up by Benedict, is the apogee of goodness, reason, and love. God's power isn't severed from God's reason and goodness. Thomas retained the inner connection between God's reason, justice, and love and the manner in which God wills. God's omnipotence remains, but he is bound in ways accessible to human reason through the workings of grace. God's will is just, insisted Aquinas. It follows that God can do nothing contrary to his nature and to what he has ordained. God's ordained power offers a world that is stable and knowable: God will not pull the rug out from under us.

A brief aside here: Although the gravamen of Benedict's address does not lie here, there are political implications deriving from views of God's power analogized from God's sovereignty to that of princes. So, even as there is a limit to the actualization of God's omnipotence, there is a limit to the rule of any prince in the Thomistic system. Although the Roman dictum held that the prince is the sole legislator, this superiority is not of an arbitrary sort, for "the natural and rational order of justice...limits the sovereignty of particular states." No single human legislator can compass

---

[1] Francis Oakley, Review of *Divine Power and Possibility in St. Peter Damian's "De divina omnipotentia,"* by Irven Michael Resnick (Leiden, 1992), in *Speculum* 69, 3 (1994): 881. For more on this subject, see Oakley, "The Absolute and Ordained Power of God in Sixteenth- and Seventeenth-Century Theology," *Journal of the History of Ideas* 59, 3 (1998): 437–61.

the totality of things, spiritual and secular. There are multiple powers, and the power of each is ordained, not absolute. The king's powers derive from law. A king cannot just do anything he pleases: his power is ordained, hence limited. The king must "bridle himself to avoid *iniuria*, for his function as minister and vicar of God requires him to act in accordance with law." The king's status is not above or outside the law, no more than God's power puts him in a realm altogether outside his creation. The king must be under the law. It follows that the king's sovereignty "was essentially judicial and executive"; the king was not set "above the law."[2]

My main point here is that the authority of the prince is bound: his will is not and cannot be absolute, and there are limits to the obedience of his subjects. This is no political theory of submission, then. It would be most interesting to trace views of rulership in the Koran (the notion of the caliphate and a caliph whose fatwas have the force of absolute law with subjects bound to submit) to construals of God's divine will, limited or unlimited. Clearly, I cannot do that here, but I wanted to point out that the debate on which Benedict embarked has many facets, many strands, including those with direct implications for political governance itself.

Back to theology: Once introduced, the nominalism of Duns Scotus and his successors clings to all future projects. For some it was an unwelcome 'hanger on' that had to be argued against at every opportunity; for others it was a liberating note that broke the chokehold of medieval realism and universalism. For some theologians, it was under the canopy of God's ordained powers that an account of God's power as absolute yet self-limiting was sheltered. God was limited by what he had done. But the intelligibility of the world is more difficult to assert if one associates God's absolute power with a notion of limitlessness: *absoluta* rather than *ordinata*.

There are strong and weak versions of the thesis that holds that ordained order is contingent since God saves and damns whomever he will. The strong thesis is usually associated with nominalism, as articulated first by Duns Scotus and then by William of Ockham. A weak statement of the thesis sees more continuity than change and avers that Ockham and the nominalists were not all that different in their views of God's sovereignty from Aquinas. It would be a mistake to charge that, with Ockham, God becomes an arbitrary sovereign whose will is not bound by either intellect or law, as if that settles the matter.

---

[2] Ewart Lewis, "King above Law? 'Quod Principi Placuit' in Bracton," *Speculum* 39, 2 (1964): 258, 268.

And yet there is a shift. With Duns Scotus, the will or *voluntas* moves to center stage. Free choice applies univocally to God and man. God's absolute power is not in a realm of possibility from which God created a physical order; rather it is the ability to act outside an order that is already established. Ordinary citizens cannot act outside the established order. Sovereign powers, however, because they make the laws, can suspend them and create new laws. Similarly, God acts in accord with his ordained creation, but he also acts outside of this order as he exercises his absolute power.

By the early fourteenth century, it is common for theologians of this school to maintain that the Father has a form of absolute power that is beyond the power of the Son or the Holy Spirit. The equality of the three persons of the Trinity fades in this formulation in favor of an absolutism of God the Father. It is easy to see, though one shouldn't make it too easy, the ways in which the migration of such accounts into theories of earthly *dominium* is fraught with all sorts of implications.

That God's power is both contingent and omnipotent is, then, deepened in the work of William of Ockham, at least on the strong statements of the thesis I noted above. The challenge arises in determining where the tendency Benedict criticizes lies. For theologians prior to Ockham had also insisted that God is able to do whatever can be done that does not imply a contradiction. Ockham introduces a note of contingency into the picture: thus, for example, God can save a person utterly lacking in charity, and by his power two bodies can exist in the same place at the same time. Created nature does not constrain the power of God fully, any more than an established system of laws constrains a truly sovereign ruler. In the world of medieval realism, the freely willing human being was fundamentally rational and could be brought to will the good. After nominalism, holding this becomes altogether more difficult.

Once the structure of medieval Thomism starts to crack, God's omnipotence leaves human beings stewing in a kind of permanent impotence as their agency is swamped by God's arbitrary power or, alternatively, human free willing and capacity to 'do' shrinks the realm of divine agency as sovereign selves go to work. The will of an all-powerful God is the ultimate cause of things. We cannot come to know this God with any degree of certainty. Nothing lies in between God's will and the countless individuals that exist in time and space. There is no intelligible world or any free order in nature that we can discern. Whatever Ockham and those who followed him believed they were doing in invoking God's absolute power, the fallout, then and, as we have seen, now, is fraught with difficulties.

It is the shift from *logos* to will that Benedict resists, pointing out, correctly, that the shift to will in Western theology takes on many of the features of the view of God as will, not reason, that he criticizes in Islam via his Byzantine interlocutor. This is an open invitation to a dialogue concerning deep theological differences and whether there are possibilities within Islam for bringing God closer to *Logos*. That was not, at least not initially, the outcome. As the waters settle and cooler heads prevail, perhaps this important dialogue can go forward.

The most urgent issue at hand for Benedict is violence—specifically, the use of violence to coerce belief or the use of belief to spur violence, such as religiously motivated terrorism. Let me add one thing here before we turn to Benedict's central points. It is very difficult for many contemporary observers in the West to credit the religious motivation behind Islamist extremism. Highly secularized intellectuals have for so long treated ideas as epiphenomenal, in the conviction that whatever motivates people politically is, at rock bottom, about economics or crude power, that they dismiss the arguments people themselves give for why they are doing what they are doing.

Yet in fatwa after fatwa Osama bin Laden, and not he alone, has made it abundantly clear that the Prophet, in his view, demands that all Jews ("Jewish dogs" to be specific), Christians, and infidels be killed whenever and wherever they may be found and that coerced conversion is entirely acceptable. Those who do not submit are to be killed. He has stated, in fatwa after fatwa, that Muslims are called to jihad, violent jihad, against Muslims who do not accept his views and against all non-Muslims generally. (As we know, Hindu and Shinto contractors and laborers in Iraq have been captured and slaughtered as infidels.) He makes no bones about it. Why can Western experts not accept these as the motivations for al-Qaeda terrorism? It says something about the secularization of the West that religion must be reduced in significance, and it is enormously patronizing to boot.

So my second task is to take seriously these evocations of violence. Let's take the Islamists at their word. How does the Christian respond? How do other Muslims respond? Although Benedict indicated he was "deeply sorry for the reactions in some countries to a few passages of [his] address," he did not back down on his central themes or on his call for a "frank and sincere dialogue with great mutual respect." As I indicated at the outset, that dialogue cannot go forward in an atmosphere of violence and intimidation or, I would add, when Muslims can, and have, built over 2,000 mosques in the United States but no Christian community can build a single church in the kingdom of Saudi Arabia. These conditions do not permit the open preaching of faith and the ecumenical engagements that a commitment to reason and non-violence requires.

Benedict traces the vagaries of the separation of reason and faith in the West with the progressive "de-Hellenization of Christianity," culminating with Kant's setting thinking aside "in order to make room for faith" and in the liberal theology of the nineteenth century. But one need not stand down from reason in order to make room for faith. This, for Benedict, is a fundamental mistake. We made a further mistake when we became so enamored of the extraordinary successes in the natural and physical sciences that a particular scientific model and epistemology, positivism, seemed the only way to engage in truly scientific and critical thinking. Trying to model everything in this way meant, once again, that any question of faith or defense of "moral values" got reduced to subjectivism. So we wound up with what the philosopher Charles Taylor has called a pretty crummy deal: narrow positivism and epistemologically indefensible subjectivism.

The true way of faith, for Benedict, stitches together reason and faith: In the beginning was *Logos*. To this end, we must broaden our "concept of reason and its application," for "reason and faith" must "come together in a new way" (#56). We cannot limit reason to that which is empirically verifiable. This is why theology belongs in our institutions of higher learning and as one of the human sciences. This is no longer just an 'academic' matter but an issue of the greatest urgency to our time. What is urgently required now more than ever is a dialogue, Benedict warns, especially between Islam and 'the West,' which is usually a stand-in for 'Christianity,' though many in the West do not want to put it that way precisely because they prefer to downplay religion, not a terribly promising way to begin such a dialogue.

In Benedict's words, "A reason which is deaf to the divine and which relegates religion into the realm of subcultures is incapable of entering into the dialogue of cultures" (#58). Now, if all of us can accept the many advances of modern science, we have to accept the "rational structures of nature as a given" (#59), or how else could science have accomplished so much that is so stunning? This, in turn, should tell us that there is a warrant in nature for a strong commitment to reason. Because God is the author of nature, it follows that God has created a universe knowable and known to us. How can we then act in ways that demean and downgrade reason if God himself is its author?

This, at least, is the ground on which one might start a dialogue. In the West, we have suffered harm by becoming averse to "questions which underlie" (#62) our own commitment to rationality in so many things. Correlatively, it is clear that Benedict believes only harm can come if the variant of Islam that prevails in our time is one that sees in God a voluntarist and even capricious power to which we are bound to submit without question and in which reason plays no role. I am not expert enough to explore what resources lie within Islam that might recuperate a strong role for reason and soften at least somewhat the highly voluntarist strain that we are all familiar with.

Of this much I am certain: The deep theological issues will not be settled anytime soon, if ever. But might we not do at least this much (for Christians it would be both principle and pragmatism involved with faithful Muslims finding their own grounds): namely, reject violence deployed in the name of the triumph of a faith. Christians did this a long, long time ago; indeed, Christians have done so many mea culpas by now concerning historic instances in which their faith served as an occasion for violence that it is no longer clear to me that further apologies do any good. After a time, these mea culpas begin to take on the sickly characteristics of self-abasement. Finally, the proof of the pudding is in the eating.

Might it be possible that Christians and Muslims could prescind on the understanding of God as *Logos* and come together on the practical, concrete grounds of rejecting violence? From the Muslim end, this would require a rejection of al-Qaeda and Islamist radicalism. It would mean that fatwas calling Muslims to slaughter in the name of Allah would need to be answered strongly and in no uncertain terms in order to demonstrate a commitment to non-violence.

Christians, in turn, would need to take every opportunity to reaffirm a commitment to not using faith as a goad to achieve religiously affirmed ends and to do everything in their power to be supportive of their Muslim brethren who are taking the path away from radical Islamism. As to what form that support might take, here Christians should be guided by others and not simply assume that they know what is best for the Muslim community, whether in their own societies or more generally. Many citizens, myself included, were saddened by the muted nature of the response by leaders of the Muslim community in America at the time of 9/11. Where were the strong voices of denunciation? There were Muslims who criticized imams on this score, and many found themselves under threat by radicalized Muslims in their communities. (I know this personally, including a death threat so serious that a professor acquaintance of mine was not permitted to leave his home for travel for months. Even this did not prevent his endangerment as shots were fired into his home study.

These threats came from Wahhabist-inflamed radicals here in America.) So this will not be easy. We should not underestimate the barriers within the Muslim community to the path here called for. It is all the more important that Christians not erect their own barriers to this effort.

There are many groups, some explicitly Christian and some not, that are pushing for this dialogue. For example, in the United Kingdom a manifesto was issued recently that indicated one of its aims was to "empower moderate and secular Muslim groups in the UK with the political tools and campaigning knowledge they need to take the fight to the extremists, mosque by mosque, university campus by university campus, street corner by street corner." To this end, they indicate they will find a way to provide space and support for moderate Muslims to come together and to share ideas with others who have faced a similar struggle against extremists. This is one explicitly political way to go. But there are other avenues, quieter and less explicitly political ones, to promote the way of deep engagement and dialogue that Benedict embraces.

And by all means in this process let us not assume that there will be a complete rapprochement on any of these matters. It is often quite unhelpful to speak of the "three Abrahamic faiths" as if they blur together, for this is not the case. The distinctions and differences are there, and they should not be discounted. But can they be reasoned about? Only, Benedict tells us, if we accept the underlying rationality of the universe, of nature herself. In Islam, the primary track taken post-prophet in the area of what in the West we call theology has in fact been jurisprudence, various schools of legal interpretation, since Islam is a law-based religion in a way Christianity is not. Surely there is a major opening here to a discussion of the grounds of reason, else how can one form of jurisprudence be seen as superior or more compelling than another unless one gets into an endless fight about which school is somehow closer to the prophet?

Today's jihadism is bound up with the identification of God as absolutely will and command, even commanding that which is irrational. Are there grounds in Islam to argue against a voluntarist concept of the nature of God? There surely must be; there surely are. Let these voices be heard and be brought forward not only to counter the Islamists but to engage robustly in the dialogue Benedict has so brilliantly launched. The search for a language in which to conduct the necessary dialogue will go on. Surely, however, there can be no more powerful or compelling ground than, first, the acknowledgment that God is *Logos* and, second, that reason, hence faith, cannot countenance slaying others to promote a holy war or other 'faith' end.

To this end, it is indeed a hopeful sign that a month following Benedict's Regensburg Lecture, thirty-eight Islamic leaders published an "Open Letter" to the pope in which they embraced his call for an intellectually serious engagement between Muslims and Christians. More important, they rejected the extremist interpretation that jihad means an obligatory holy war of conquest. In somewhat muted language, though the reference point was surely clear, they condemned those who "have disregarded a long and well-established tradition in favor of utopian dreams where the end justifies the means," and they did this in a free-lance manner, absent "the sanction of God, His Prophet, or the learned tradition."[3] What this shows us and tells us is that openly aired difference and clear critique are not barriers to ecumenical dialogue and encounter. We show far more respect for those from faiths different from our own when we air our differences rather than pretending everything is hunky-dory and we all pretty much agree. We do not. But does that mean some of us must kill the others of us until all "submit to the will of Allah," as the Islamists would have it? God forbid. The God of reason and love forbids.

Benedict XVI ascended to the papacy in a parlous time. In Europe we see the exhaustion of the faith, the loss of hope, a culture of materialism, a culture that refuses to bear children, a kind of soft nihilism. If the only thing holding you together is the euro and if you cannot mount a robust defense of that human dignity that underwrites your commitment to fundamental human rights, then you are on the grounds of despair and cultural exhaustion. When hard extremism comes up against soft nihilism, I think we know which will win. But it's a rotten bargain all the way around. Benedict faces the formidable task of reminding Europe of who she really is and asking her to engage in a profound project of recuperation, a revival of Christian culture at its very best combined with a profound recognition of the many blessings Christianity conferred, including a culture that sustains endless self-scrutiny and criticism.

At the same time, Europe—a Europe that can be revivified—faces daunting challenges from a dangerous extremism aided and abetted by a non-extremist majority who are nonetheless mightily turned off by the soft nihilism of the countries in which they find themselves. I have to believe that it isn't a fundamental human rights respective of human dignity that they object to, or basic constitutionalism (it would be a horror if majorities in Muslim immigrant communities in the West believed that) but, rather, a

---

[3] "Open Letter to the Pope" by 38 Muslim leaders, 13 October 2006, http://ammanmessage.com/media/openLetter/english.pdf.

hedonistic reductive materialism that should not be conflated with Western culture *tout court*. It is only when the West remembers her Christian heritage, when Christians, for heaven's sake, remember this, that a deep, candid dialogue can go forth.

This need for (Christian) memory made the response in many Christian quarters to Benedict's address so dispiriting. Rather than tackling the fundamental questions Benedict raised, many expressed chagrin and disappointment that he had raised those questions in the first place! Somehow we are never to upset anyone. But real engagements are upsetting. They are bound to be. We cannot avoid that. Rather than cringing and hiding and "making nice" in a way that doesn't credit people with holding the strong beliefs that they hold, we should forthrightly set out our own understanding and ask our interlocutors to help us understand correctly if we've got it wrong or to let us know what is going on that would invite, for example, a stress on a hyper-voluntarist understanding of God that negates *Logos* in the process. That is the only way dignified human beings can conduct an honest dialogue.

Benedict no doubt had to express his sorrow at the reaction spurred by extremists stirring up "the streets" against him but, thankfully, he did not apologize for his comments, as he should not. Any charitable reader recognizes immediately that Benedict's address is a call to reason, not resentment; to engagement, not withdrawal; to ecumenism, not triumphalism. Christians of every denomination would do well to stand with him. These are questions that will haunt our lifetimes and beyond. We will be judged to a great extent in the eyes of history on how we have engaged these vital questions, and we owe Benedict a huge debt of thanks for his contribution.

American Nominalism and Our Need for the Science of Theology

Peter Augustine Lawler

My purpose here is to show how Pope Benedict XVI's defense of a true science of theology applies to the United States of America. That defense is, finally, of the reasonableness of belief in a personal God who is rational, creative, and erotic. It requires going beyond the Regensburg Lecture to the pope's pathbreaking encyclical on love and to places in his writings where he makes clear that the fundamental human choice is not so much between reason and revelation as between the impersonal *Logos*, or God of the classical philosophers, and the personal *Logos*, or God described by the early Christians. The argument concerning which of those reasonable choices is more reasonable was what animated the study of the science of theology in the time of Hellenic Christianity. For us Americans, the greatness and the relevance of this philosopher-theologian-pope are in his articulation of a theory or science commensurate with the great practical achievement of our Founders, who, as the American Catholic political thinker John Courtney Murray claimed, built better than they knew. I'm dispensing with formality here, hoping to speak plainly what I see as the truth. In my effort to do so, I gratefully acknowledge a debt to Joseph Ratzinger, Pope Benedict XVI, that couldn't be captured by any number of footnotes.*

* Here's what I read by Ratzinger/Benedict to prepare for writing this essay: the Regensburg Lecture, the encyclical on love, *Introduction to Christianity* (San Francisco: Ignatius, 1994), *In the Beginning...A Catholic Understanding of the Story of Creation and the Fall* (Grand Rapids, Mich.: Eerdmans, 2005), and most of the writings and speeches contained in *The Essential Pope Benedict XVI*, ed. John Thornton and Susan Varenne (New York: HarperCollins, 2007). Particularly important in shaping my argument here from *The Essential Pope Benedict XVI* was "On the Theological Basis of Prayer and Liturgy" (Chap. 19) and "Truth and Freedom" (Chap. 35).

Even though the modern world has been characterized by de-Christianization and de-Hellenization, that doesn't mean it's fundamentally anti-Christian or anti-Greek. We speak more of the dignity or autonomy of the human person than ever. And we certainly have more confidence in and are more dependent on the science we've inherited from the Greeks than ever. Modern de-Hellenization has been largely animated by the desire to free the willful God and willful human person made in his image from being distorted or annihilated in the impersonal metaphysical system of Aristotle or some other philosopher or scientist. Modern de-Christianization has been largely animated by the desire to free science from all anthropomorphic or personal distortion in order to fuel real progress toward a certain understanding of the genuinely universal structure of reality, the goal of science first articulated, quite imperfectly, by the classical Greek philosophers. De-Christianization has been pursued on behalf of the free person, and de-Hellenization, on behalf of impersonal science. They have been operating simultaneously and at cross-purposes.

The truth is that our world is in some ways both more personal and more impersonal, more Christian and more Greek, than ever. The distance between our personal experiences and what we think we know through science has never been wider. Without admitting it, we've abandoned the true goal of science, which is to give an account of the way all things, including human beings, are. We don't really believe we can reason about the true situation of the only being in the world, the human person, who is open to the truth about nature. We think we can know everything but the being who can know. We don't deny that such a personal being exists, whatever our scientists may teach. We don't even begin to try to lose our puny selves in some impersonal system or pantheistic reverie. Such denial is for Buddhists, with their amazing self-discipline. For now the phrase "Western Buddhist" remains an oxymoron.

It's especially clear that we Americans now see ourselves both more personally and more impersonally than ever. Virtually all sophisticated Americans claim to believe that Darwin teaches the whole truth about who or what we are. For Darwin, the individual human being exists only to serve the human species. Even our super-smart species has no enduring significance in the accidental evolutionary process. It's true both that I'm nothing but species fodder and that what I, in particular, do has less than negligible significance for our species' future. Natural selection depends on the average, anonymous behavior of a huge number of members of any particular species. The individual or person and his illusory concerns about his personal significance mean or are nothing. Even the genes that I so dutifully spread are soon dispersed into insignificance.

The same sophisticated Americans who pride themselves on being whole-hog Darwinians speak incessantly about the freedom and dignity of the individual and are proud of their freedom to choose. The particularly modern source of pride remains personal freedom from all authority, including the authority of God and nature. Our professed confidence in the reality of that freedom may be stronger than ever today. Even our neo-Darwinian scientists, such as Daniel Dennett, who think there's no foundation for the idea of human dignity in what we know through science, admit it would be a disaster if they could really convince us to stop taking our dignity seriously. Certainly one piece of evidence that we're not living in genuinely reasonable times is that most sophisticated Americans seem unable to join Dennett in recognizing the laughable contradiction in their official self-understanding as autonomous chimps.

We Americans, in fact, are so unscientific that we don't even try to account for what we can see with our own eyes. Culturally speaking, we're divided into Darwin affirmers and Darwin deniers, into those who say that his theory of evolutionary natural selection can explain everything and those who say it explains nothing. Anybody should be able to see that the truth lies somewhere in between those two extremes.

The Darwin affirmers provide the best evidence around today that what Darwin teaches couldn't possibly be completely true. They tend to think of themselves so thoroughly as autonomous individuals that often they don't seek the natural fulfillment that comes through spreading their genes, through having kids. They're not doing their duty to their species by generating their replacements. They're even doing everything they can in the most scientific way not to have to be replaced. They think being itself will be extinguished if and when they die. Can Darwin explain why healthy members of a species enjoying the most favorable of environments would suddenly and quite consciously just decide to stop reproducing? It seems that members of a species smart enough and curious enough to have discovered the theory of natural selection are acting to make that theory untrue.

Meanwhile, our Evangelical and orthodox believers come much closer to living the way nature intends for our species to flourish. They pair-bond or marry, have lots of kids, raise them well, and then step aside for their natural replacements without inordinate resistance. What the Evangelicals and Mormons believe is better for our species' future than what the neo-Darwinians believe. Examining this behavior, a neo-Darwinian genuinely concerned for our species' future might insist that evolution not be taught in our schools. Nor can our sociobiologists explain why those Americans who believe that, as persons made in the image of a supernatural God, their true home is somewhere else are most at home in this world as citizens, friends, neighbors, parents, and children.

Still, our Evangelicals tend to join both those who speak of their autonomy and our Darwinians in believing that there's no support in nature at all for their purpose-driven lives. If it weren't for the absolute truth of the Bible, they assert, something like aimless or relativistic naturalism would be true. They often present the human choice as between two competing worldviews, and reason has little to say about how to make that choice. Our Evangelicals often give themselves far too little credit. Their criticism of our libertarian autonomy freaks and our Darwinians would retain plenty of force even if they lost faith in the God of the Bible.

Our libertarians, our Darwinians, and our Evangelicals all agree that there is no science of theology. Reason, they insist, can't give us any understanding on who or what God is in a way that would provide actual guidance for our lives. They don't believe that we're hardwired, so to speak, to know the *Logos* who, or which, is the source of our freedom and our openness to the truth about all things. Libertarians and Evangelicals both believe that the free person is real, but they don't believe that there's any support in nature for his existence. Darwinians, quite unrealistically, deny what anyone can see with his own eyes about personal or individual behavior. Because we all refuse to believe in the possibility of a science of theology, we all lack a way of talking reasonably about the real lives of particular human persons.

We don't live in a very reasonable time because we're governed by a particular cultural or historical choice to limit the domain of reason over our lives. This modern self-limitation, as I'll explain, was quite understandable. But we now know from experience that the simultaneous attempts to free faith from science or philosophy and science from faith have produced undignified, self-mutilated lives. Most fundamentally, we seem not to be courageous enough to live well with what we know. The truth is that the modern view of reason is quite questionable. It is, thank God, far from the last word on what we can know.

The Science of Theology: Hellenic Christianity versus Classical Philosophy

To free us from the delusion that we have that last word on reason, we return to the first words about the relationship between Greek philosophy or science and Christianity spoken during the period of Hellenic Christianity. Then, the Greeks and the Christians agreed that we're hardwired as beings with minds to think about who or what God must be and that we're animated by *eros*, or love, to seek the truth about God. The idea that God is *Logos* is what allowed the Greeks and the Christians to use both argument and mockery to collaborate against those religions that are obviously unreasonable and man-made. God is neither cruel nor arbitrary, and the truth about God must correspond to what we can know about ourselves and the rest of nature according to our best lights. Both the Greeks and the Christians contributed to genuine enlightenment, to the liberation of human beings from the confines of merely civil or political theology, from a world where the word of God both was used as a weapon and justified the use of weapons.

Through reflection, Aristotle attempted to grasp God as the object of every human desire or love. He understood God only as the *object* of love, as a wholly self-sufficient or unerotic or unmovable being, not as a person at all. Aristotle's God is certainly not a "relational" God, one who cares or even knows about the existence of particular human beings. According to Aristotle, our pursuit of divine knowledge, or what God knows, becomes progressively more impersonal. The pursuit of philosophic or scientific truth requires that the individual philosopher die to himself. The Socratic drama of the pursuit of wisdom is the particular being losing himself in his apprehension of anonymous or impersonal truth.

From this view, we approach divinity, or what is best in us, through our perception of the *logos* or rational causality that governs all things. We see past every anthropomorphic claim for personal intervention or personal causation that would disrupt that *logos*. From this liberated view, the idea of a personal God is an oxymoron. It is, in fact, a repulsive denial of the responsibility of theological science and science generally.

The Christian criticism of Aristotelian theology is that it doesn't account for what we really know about the human person. For the Greek philosophers, the realm of human freedom, finally, is a mythical idea, one that must be rhetorically supported but for which there's no scientific evidence. The only freedom is the freedom of the human mind from anthropomorphic delusions about natural causation. The Christians respond that human longings and human action exhibit evidence of personal freedom, and the person must have some actual foundation in being itself. What we do know, they say, points in the direction of the creative activity of a personal God. The personalities of God and man can't be wholly or irredeemably unrelated. The possibility of the free and rational being open to the truth depends upon the corresponding possibility of a personal, rational science of theology.

The classical philosophers were, of course, perfectly aware that human beings are "manly," that they need to feel important. Such self-confidence is required to make self-conscious life endurable and great human deeds possible. But according to their science, all assertions of human importance are unrealistic exaggerations, and the philosopher gently mocks without obviously undermining the aspirations of particular individuals to self-sufficiency. For the Christians, however, even science depends upon the possibility of personal significance, and Christian theology criticizes both the civil theology and the natural theology of the Greeks and Romans for their inability to account for personal freedom: for the being who is not fundamentally merely part of a city or part of some necessitarian natural whole. According to the Christians, not only do particular men and women need to feel important; they are, in fact, important. The Christians add that the unrealistic exaggerations of their magnanimous pretensions need, in fact, the chastening of the truthful virtue of humility, the virtue of ineradicably relational and lovingly dependent beings.

That there's a ground for personal freedom in an otherwise seemingly necessitarian cosmos does, in some ways, offend the mind, but to understand all that exists in terms of impersonal causation suggests that Being itself is constituted by an intelligence that is incapable of comprehending itself. The being who can understand Being, the human being, seems to be a chance occurrence in a cosmos that has no particular need for and is seemingly distorted by his existence. The appearance of the human person, even the philosopher with the name Socrates, necessarily offends the human mind in some ways, but as far as we know, the human mind can only appear or function in a whole person. The real existence of the whole philosopher or physicist can't be accounted for in any mathematical or certainly necessitarian physics. So in some ways it might offend the person's reason less to affirm an account of the precondition and ground of all being to be creative and truly conscious, or erotic and rational, thinking. The world, in the final analysis, is more love than mathematics, and the particular human person is more significant and wonderful than the stars.

The Greeks focus on the eternity, the Christians on the loving creativity of God. For the Christians, the God who is the ultimate source of our being is animated, as we are, by *logos* and *eros*. The source of our being is someone who can't be reduced to mind or will or even some theoretical combination of the two. Made in his image, we personal, erotic, and knowing beings can't be reduced to mind or will or body or even some abstract combination of the three. One aspect of the reasonableness of faith is its perception of the intrinsic link between God's love and the whole reality of human life.

The philosophic or scientific understanding of the world in terms of impersonal necessity or eternity alone can't account for the real existence of persons, of beings open to the truth and defined in this world by time. The eternal God of the Greeks has no relationship to the temporal, and the dependence and incompleteness of time-bound beings mean nothing to him. Insofar as human beings are moved by his existence, it is in pursuit of self-sufficient freedom from who they really are. If time and eternity really are infinitely distant from one another, then we can't understand why human beings can know God or anything eternal.

Classical monotheism, in truth, denies the real relationships between God and man and between eternity and time. It may, in fact, culminate in the conclusion that the only thing a human being can know for certain is that he's not eternal, that he's some kind of chance occurrence soon to be extinguished in a necessitarian cosmos. Greek philosophers clearly distinguished the personal illusion of religion from the philosophic science of theology, showing that, for the most part, at least the lives of particular men are as unreal or as insignificant as the personal gods they invent. For the Greeks, religion was useful for the regulation of lives, but it has nothing to do with the truth.

From the Greek view, the early Christians seemed like atheists. They rejected the whole world of ancient religion and its gods as nothing but empty custom or contrary to what we can really know. That's because the Christians agreed with the Greek philosophers that traditional myth must be rejected in favor of the truth about Being, and the Christians added that all human beings are called to regulate their lives in light of what they can really know. Only from the perspective of a personal *logos* can the truth affirm and guide human freedom. The Christians, by discovering a transformed understanding of the *Logos* at the ground of Being, showed God to be a person concerned with persons. The Christians show why divine truth can't be separated from personal morality.

From the perspective of the distinctive reasonableness of Christian faith, man's inner openness to God comes from what he knows about himself as a relational being, as a person who knows and loves other "whos." The philosophical view of God is that our thoughts or minds alone are divine, and the mind detached from the whole human being is less a who than a what. The Christian view is that we're made in God's image as whole rational and erotic beings; not just thought but love is divine. The standard of moral judgment is what we can't help but know about our personhood or creatureliness, about the responsibilities that flow from personal awareness of loving dependence. Sin flows from the denial of the truth about our free-dom, from the madness that flows from the aspiration to be as autonomous or self-sufficient as some thinkers imagine God to be. The sin described in Genesis flows from the false separation of divine wisdom from personal or "relational" morality.

In the Hellenic world, the science of theology was always reasonable without achieving rational certainty. The truth is that the arguments for the Christian and the Greek accounts of the *logos* at the ground of Being both have problems. Christianity's view that what we can know about the human person reasonably points in the direction of a personal *logos* doesn't eradicate the apparent *mystery* of personal freedom in a world seemingly governed by natural necessity. If the mystery is real, the Greek philosophers argued, science becomes impossible. The Christian response that without that mystery there would be nobody to know scientific truth doesn't com-pletely answer that objection. Nor could the Christians dispel all questions about why a wholly self-sufficient and rational God completely ungov-erned by time and chance would become a Creator. How can it be that such a God is erotic or animated by a passionate sense of incompleteness?

And, of course, some Christians wondered whether the Hellenizing of Christianity through the emphasis on God as *Logos* chained him, in effect, to natural laws that weren't his creation. The emphasis on either God's love or God's reason can easily seem to compromise the freedom of His will and so the omnipotence on which our hopes for personal salvation rest. Argu-ably that emphasis also undermined the freedom of the will of the persons made in his image. The limiting of the willful God with either *logos* or love seems to undermine his personal significance, and so ours.

Modern Nominalism

It's understandable why there were Christian efforts to liberate God from science, from the constraints of reason. The most obvious efforts came from late-medieval nominalism. Words are names, nothing more, it as-serted. Our speech, or *logos*, doesn't give us access to the way God or nature is. The word of God is pure will, and the word of man, who is made in his image, is also pure will. Words, for us, are merely weapons because we're not hardwired to discover the truth about God, nature, or each other through reason. This nominalist conclusion was, in effect, affirmed by the leaders of the Reformation. They, too, meant to free the personal experi-ence of the living God from the cold constraints of reason. Our direct (really, private) personal experience of his will and his love eludes every impersonal system. The living, giving God, the Reformers believed, is nothing like Aristotle's God.

By freeing the person from *logos*, the combined effects of voluntarism and the Reformation were to deny the possibility of a science of theology. And so they also freed science from any concern with God, allowing it to focus exclusively on what we can know with certainty, the mathematically expressed laws of matter in motion. To know with certainty is to know without any personal distortion. Modern science becomes more openly impersonal than its ancient predecessor because Aristotelian theology left too much room for science's personal distortion and directed the mind toward uncertain speculation. The aim of modern physics, ultimately, is the same as that of ancient physics, to show that the world is the home of the human mind.

Now we can finally turn to how the nominalist denial of the science of theology shaped the early modern liberalism, the Lockeanism, that, in turn, shaped both the American founding and the individualistic dynamic of American history. For Locke, we experience ourselves as free individuals or persons, but there is no divine or natural support for our personhood or individuality. Nature is utterly indifferent to my personal existence, so I have to establish my personal significance, my very being as a free individual, in opposition to that indifference. From my individual view, nature is worthless, and according to nature, I'm worthless.

The detachment of the person from nature or from *logos*, in the name of freedom and in the name of science, allows us to experience ourselves as pure freedom or pure selfishness. There's no evidence, in fact, for an active or giving Creator, no evidence that God or nature provides for the person in any way. Our personal freedom, like God's, is utterly mysterious: there's no evident natural or divine foundation for *me*, for my being. So I have to establish and expand my freedom— my very being—on my own, through my own willful work. I have to create or constitute myself out of nothing, as God allegedly created the whole world.

Like the Christians and against the Greeks, we Americans assert that each particular person is equally and infinitely significant. From the perspective of the person, from my perspective, nothing is more important than the security, significance, and happiness that characterize *my* existence. Each person or individual exists for himself, not genuinely in a dependent and loving relationship with others. Love of God or other human persons is for suckers. It's undignified for me not to tell the truth about how contingent and self-determined my own being is.

The idea of God remains in Locke in the form of Deism, which is, in part, a revival of the ancient rejection of an active, personal God. Locke's "Nature's God" is a past-tense God. Deism also has some connection with the Pascalian view of the mysterious hiddenness of God. Certainly Locke's God is not quite the impersonal God of Aristotle, because the former's affirmation of the reality of the mystery of the free human person points in some sense to a mysterious Creator. But that Creator does not show himself as a person to us. We act as suckers when we think of ourselves as creatures, as in some way gratefully dependent on or personally connected to his providence. Our Lockean Declaration of Independence, we remember, speaks of a Creator but never of creatures.

For Locke, words, our capacity for reasonable speech or *logos*, don't give us any access to the truth about nature or God. There is, in fact, no science of theology. Words are the weapons we use to secure our being against nature and without a providential God. Words are the weapons we use to make ourselves progressively freer or progressively more real. Locke's state of nature, for example, was not meant to be an empirical account of the way human beings are. It distorts and exaggerates our personal or individual freedom. The state of nature was a tool used by Locke to liberate the individual from nature and from other individuals.

The Lockean individual is itself a weapon, a willful invention abstracted from the whole, relational truth about the human person. Proof of our freedom is our power to make that abstraction more real over time. Locke himself was all for limited government, but his project was hardly limited to government. He aimed, with great success, to reconstruct every human relationship and institution with the free or selfishly calculating individual in mind. As the Supreme Court said in *Lawrence v. Texas*, our Framers deliberately gave the word *liberty* no definite, stable content so that it could be used as a weapon for each generation of Americans to advance the cause of individual liberation or autonomy. What seems like necessary and proper limits to liberty to one generation of Americans seems like despotism to the next. Marriage, we now are coming to think, is a free contract between any two individuals for any purpose at all; it has been freed from any necessary connection to our biological purposes and limitations.

Locke's individual is free to view the wholly impersonal or mathematical nature that the scientists can comprehend and control as a resource for their personal disposal. He is even free to think of his own body in that way. His view of his freedom from nature even allows him to be critical scientifically of the impersonal pretensions of science. If it's true that there's no necessary connection between the free, willful individual and the natural order, then there's no reason to believe that we can comprehend the order of nature except by bringing it under our personal control.

Locke to Marx: History Replaces Nature

Freeing the person from nature necessarily personalizes what we can actually know about nature. We can only know what we have made in our own image. The purpose of our reason is to will personal reality into being. So all science, all human knowledge, must finally be technological; technology or history, the names we give to what we have made for ourselves, even seems to be all there is. The detachment of the person from nature frees the individual to impose his desire for personal significance on nature. We are free to replace impersonal natural evolution, which means nothing to us, with conscious and volitional evolution, human effort with the indefinite perpetuation of each infinitely significant individual in mind. And the science of theology, which aims at orthodoxy, is replaced by orthopraxis; there is no truth but who and what we have made for ourselves.

It's a pretty small step from Locke to Marx, from the view that the individual is free to constitute himself to the "historical" view that he's free to constitute all there is. The detachment of science from all concern with theology eventually seems to lead to the replacement of natural science by historical science, to Marx's description of the impending total victory of human freedom over nature and God. The separation of eternity (impersonal natural science) from time (the free person or individual) at the beginning of the modern world is resolved, according to Marx, by the victory of time. Human freedom or history frees each of us from the tyranny of the indifference of eternal necessity.

There are many problems with this conclusion. To begin with, if history is a *science*, then *logos* once again seems to reign at the expense of the freedom or significance of particular persons. It doesn't matter what I really intend to do; my personal actions only have significance as part of a whole, a historical future, beyond my comprehension and control. Those who really believed history is a science were all too ready to sacrifice today's individuals for a historical perfection nobody living will ever see or enjoy. From a Lockean view, those who gave their lives to history were suckers, and those who were murdered on behalf of history were denied their personal dignity.

The tyranny of Marxists can be traced to the detachment of the abstraction "history" from the lives of particular persons or individuals. As history became a scientific replacement for modern natural science, it became just as impersonal or systematic as modern science. Hegel and Marx even wrote of "the end of history," of history as a time-bound *logos* of temporal beings. The great Marxist/Heglian Alexandre Kojève explained that the end of history would have to be the end of "man properly so-called," the disappearance of the personal being free from nature's domination. The end of history, according to Kojève, would be the victory of eternity over the temporary aberration of time. The human species would be reintegrated into nature with all the others, and there would be no one left to know the truth about the impersonal natural necessity that would once again be the truth and nothing but.

To be fair to Marx (as opposed to being fair to Marxist tyrants), he, quite incoherently, thought that the end of history or communism would be the free flourishing of individuality unconstrained by natural necessity or any other form of alienation. It's hard to know why Marx called communism *communism*, because in such a society we would be completely free from all relational obsessions, such as love, that would limit our freedom. The freedom won by human beings from nature and from each other under communism would remain, with the addition of liberation from the division of labor, from being compelled to work for others. Under communism, freedom would be just another word for nothing left that we *have* to do.

Our most astute libertarians today are beginning to see that Marx is their friend once he is stripped of insane and dangerous hopes such as the inevitability of revolution and the actual end of history. The world he worked for is the one today's libertarians celebrate as having largely arrived—the one with a huge and ever-expanding menu of choices for liberated individuals. Marx thought capitalism liberated women to be wage slaves just like men. Our libertarians tweak that observation by saying women are now free to seek self-fulfillment however they please, just like men, and the opportunities for work from which they have to choose are often challenging and enjoyable. There is no denying, in fact, that the achievements of modern technology in liberating lots of ordinary persons from scarcity and drudgery are wonderful revelations about what free beings can do here and now to improve their conditions.

Marx and our libertarians agree that the technological conquest of scarcity liberates the individual for "a menu of choices." But that liberation from God, nature, and even other people means that the personal is deprived of all guidance about how to choose. All choice that doesn't concern survival becomes a preference, a whim, so our freedom becomes nothing more than anarchy or pure indeterminacy. I can be anything I want to be, I say, but nothing I choose has genuine weight or significance. So the person, as the existentialists whine, comes to be seen as nothing more than an absurd leftover, an accidental aberration, from the impersonal natural necessity that governs the rest of existence.

The truth is that the person can't constitute himself out of nothing, and the abstract individual with that capability Locke invented always falls short of becoming anywhere near completely real. We can't remake all of reality in our image; the more we comprehend through control, the more we're aware of the infinite spaces that continue to elude us. The more we experience ourselves as free or disconnected individuals, the more we experience the mysterious contingency of our very beings. We still have bodies and we still die, and in fact we're more death-haunted than ever. We still can't help falling in love, though we Lockeans and Darwinians and Marxists have no idea how to talk about love. All our personal efforts to secure our beings have made us too anxious and disoriented, too lonely and personally insignificant, to be at home in the technological world we have created to replace our clearly inadequate natural home.

Nihilism or Relativism

Without any connection to a personal reality, a personal *logos*, beyond his own making, sometimes it seems that the free being can't endure. Today, we allegedly autonomous persons are so conscious of the limits of our biological existence that we seem incapable of creating anything that can stand the test of time. And in our time, Marx's historical science has been replaced by nihilism or techno-relativism. We can't even pretend to speak more than whimsically about anything that doesn't contribute to our futile efforts at survival. The only real morality we have left—morality reduced to safe sex or, more generally, safe choice—has nothing to do with the significance of the person's existence. Our proud claim that something real distinguishes the person from natural necessity seems more questionable than ever.

Nihilism is the view that what distinguishes me from the rest of nature means or is nothing. It means that "I," the particular person, am nothing. The time after the discrediting of Locke and Marx should, from one nihilistic view, belong to Darwin or to the revelation of the complete truth of his impersonal science. Sober Darwinians agree with whiny existentialists that the Lockean individual is absurd. There's no natural or real evidence for his existence. Surely it's ridiculous to claim the individual was somehow just dropped into nature to go to war against it like some crazed parasitic predator. The Darwinian adds that nature really does intend all animals, even us, to be basically happy or content. So we've acquired through natural selection instincts that produce pleasure in us when we do our duties as social beings; we have a natural moral sense. If we really were to detach ourselves from those instincts, we would condemn ourselves to the futile pursuit of happiness that ends only in death.

The Darwinian concludes that the Lockean individual—the individual free from nature—is nothing but a misery-producing delusion. Surely the Darwinian is right that nature provides us lots of guidance when it comes to happiness. It's still the case in our individualistic time that most people claim they're happiest as members of families, and our natural longings really do point most of us in the direction of doing what it takes to keep the species going. So, thoughtful Darwinians claim that they have the antidote to the nihilism of individualism. Nature gives us guidance concerning the point of our lives, and we find fulfillment and happiness in doing what we're inclined to do by nature.

But the Lockean can reasonably respond that Darwinism is nihilism. The impersonal truth is that I exist for the species, not for myself, and what I do as a particular individual means or is nothing. Darwin can't explain why members of only one species can think so abstractly and imaginatively that they conceive of themselves as individuals. Nor can Darwin explain why members of only one species are in full technological rebellion against nature. In Harvey Mansfield's analysis, the conviction that Darwin might teach the truth about the chance and necessity that govern every life might well have been the main cause of the "manliness run amok" of the twentieth century, just as it might be the cause of the biotechnology run amok of the twenty-first. People are more concerned than ever about their personal significance, their importance or status, their very being as particular persons, in our officially egalitarian time.

What we know is that the Lockean criticism of Darwin from the perspective of human freedom contains much truth. And the Darwinian criticism of Locke from the perspective of the natural goods connected with our embodiment is also largely true. Both these criticisms are true because the Lockeans and Darwinians both think too abstractly. They share the error of unrealistic abstractness because they agree that there is no natural support for human freedom. Words are not meant to give us any access to the truth about nature. For the Lockeans, they're weapons for individual preservation and flourishing, and for Darwinians they're for the preservation and flourishing of the species. We're certainly not hardwired to know any personal reality that we didn't make for ourselves, including, of course, God.

The American Need for a Science of Theology

We are, despite our proud enlightenment, much more a willful than a reasonable people. We believe that we're perfectly free to deny what we can know and even or especially to deny that we know it. We claim to be free to find it comfortable to believe that we're really autonomous chimps. We're free, we believe, to choose personal reality over scientific truth, distorting science to serve a freedom that our scientists don't acknowledge as real. But one sign of our true dignity, our true freedom as rational, erotic, creative, and relational beings, is that we still know that it's degrading to prefer comfort to truth. Our attempts to live without being moved by love and death (because they're more trouble than they're worth) mainly produce not some less-than-personal apathetic passivity but chaotic, angry disorientation.

Our Founders, our political Fathers, clearly privileged personal reality over impersonal science, and so they built better—they were more Christian—than they knew. They sometimes thought of themselves as proponents of the light of science and "Nature's God" against the monkish ignorance and superstition of Christians. But for them science served, above all, human freedom. And that freedom is nothing like the Epicurean serenity (the fruit of the rational acceptance of nature's indifference to Jefferson's personal significance) that Jefferson claimed to have privately enjoyed. Our Fathers' service to the significance of the person or the individual is what saves them from all charges of capitalism, materialism, atheism, and so forth. Surely most of our Fathers most of the time would have laughed at the Epicureans or Marxists or Darwinians who claimed that they were, in truth, slaves to forces beyond their personal control.

Americans may justly be criticized for sometimes regarding even other persons as natural resources to be exploited. But they're rarely so materialistic as to forget that it's a free being that's doing the exploiting. They can also be criticized for alienating themselves even from their own bodies, but that's because they think of themselves as something other than bodies. Our pragmatism isn't materialism, because it depends on our conviction that our freedom is somehow real. The free being who secures himself as something more than a body is the one, as Alexis de Tocqueville (author of the best book on Americans) explains, who freely pursues enjoyment but never takes time to surrender to actual, instinctual enjoyment. Americans, in a way, exhibit the extreme opposite of nihilistic behavior: They work hard to avoid the conclusion that their very being *is* nothing.

Not only that, our Fathers deliberately didn't make it clear whether the person they served is the creature described by Protestant Christians or the free individual described by Locke. Either way, they served the dignity of the person free from natural and political domination. Our Lockeans and Protestants ally against the impersonal natural science that denies the free will or free choice of the particular person or individual. Whether Protestant or Lockean, we understand ourselves as mysteriously free from nature. And either way we're way too sure that there's no science of theology.

Whether Protestant or Lockean, we can't really claim that our way of life is particularly reasonable. As Tocqueville explains, our Christianity saves us from the manliness run amok producing the view that anything might be done for some futuristic historical utopia. It also teaches us that we have moral duties in common and even that we were made for more than mere survival. But religion achieves these beneficial goals, Tocqueville adds, only by being exempted, without discussion, from our habitual critical scrutiny. Americans, in the name of moral freedom and just sanity itself, decide not to think about the most important questions concerning personal significance, including, of course, about God. So, in some deep way, both our religion and our incessant labor to secure our being seem to be diversions from what we really know. They both oppose human freedom to what we can know through science.

But what we know through science also seems to be a diversion from what we experience about our freedom. Our physicists can explain everything about the cosmos but the strange behavior of physicists. And our neo-Darwinian biologists don't even try to begin to explain their joyful discovery of the truth about all things as the product of tools for species flourishing. Everyone knows our scientists are self-forgetful and that they have little real to say about who human persons are. Certainly they can't explain why the Americans who believe that their true home is somewhere else are the ones most at home in this world or why those who say they believe that they are as at home here as members of any other species are most in rebellion against their social instincts and biological limitations.

Americans are caught between incompatible diversions because de-Hellenization has defended our freedom, our autonomy, so well against impersonal science and de-Christianization has emptied our freedom of any real or "transcendent" content. The result is that we live in unstable, disorienting, narcissistic, degrading, and impersonal times, and we wonder whether the freedom our Fathers worked so hard and well to secure is either real or worth defending. But our return to the time of the Hellenic Christians reminds us that the sundering of the person from *Logos* was a very questionable historical decision, one that artificially and futilely limited the scope of human reason. As far as we can tell, *Logos* must be personal; only persons are rational, erotic, and relational enough to be open to the truth about all things, and only persons have the significance that comes with living freely, responsibly, and lovingly with what they know. A wholly necessitarian or impersonal world of minds and bodies wouldn't be known by anyone at all.

The modern diversions are the results of thinking unrealistically or abstractly about who we and God really are. It really is true that the beginning of the cure for what ails us Americans is more science, not less. Our Holy Father points us in the direction of the theory, culminating in the science of theology, adequate to the great success of the experiment in freedom of our political Fathers.

Good and Bad De-Hellenization

Marc D. Guerra

Pope Benedict XVI's Regensburg Lecture is a remarkably thoughtful and, for that reason, unusual academic address. The Regensburg Lecture forcefully raises an important and inescapable question for the Christian college or university: What is the fundamental relationship between faith and reason and how should that relationship inform the intellectual life of an academic community? Yet as the lecture also makes clear, there is nothing narrowly academic about this question. As Benedict's deliberate and calibrated remarks about Islam and modernity reveal, the relationship of faith and reason is rightly a concern of the university *qua* university. But it is more than that, for the investigation of that question necessarily raises moral, political, religious, and philosophical questions that cut to the very heart of what is meant by civilization and to the living of a serious human life. The relationship between faith and reason accordingly is a question that should be of interest to any intellectually serious college or university.

For this very reason it is striking to note that more than half of the pope's lecture addresses the intellectual, spiritual, and moral problems that arise when reason and faith, not simply reason and revelation, are radically separated from one another. What are we to make of this fact? If nothing else, it suggests that Benedict chooses to address the question of the relationship of faith and reason not in the abstract but rather in the historical form in which that question has actually come down to us and confronts us today.

Benedict describes that historical form as the product of a sustained "programme of dehellenization" (#31). And he leaves little doubt that the results of this process are less than desirable, for reason as well as for faith. We must also observe, though, that the term *de-Hellenization* is itself a term of distinction: it describes what has gradually happened to the understanding of Christian faith over the past five hundred years. It does not positively articulate what the proper relationship of faith and reason is. Nor, for that matter, does it answer the question of whether Christian faith necessarily should be "Hellenized." Indeed, to a great degree the term begs the question of what Hellenized Christianity is in the first place.

One gains a partial understanding of what Benedict means by Helle-nization through his account of the sequential stages of de-Hellenization. He locates the first of these stages in the Reformation. Reacting to what they saw as the nearly total absorption of the teachings of the Christian faith into a predominantly alien Aristotelian framework, Reformers such as Luther and Calvin turned to the principle of *sola scriptura* in the hope of reclaiming the true content of God's revelation and the biblical way of life proclaimed by the Christ of the Gospels. By formalizing a theoreti-cally unbridgeable gap between faith and reason, the Reformers paved the way for holding the truths held by Christian faith apart from those grasped by human reason. (Benedict does note that this formulation was in a way anticipated in the thought of the late medieval exponents of nominalism such as Duns Scotus [#25].) As a result of this gap, the Reformers' account of the relation of faith and reason paradoxically in some ways resembles those given by anti-theological early modern philosophers like Spinoza.[1] Over against the decadent Scholasticism of the late Middle Ages, the Reformers framed the question of faith and reason in such a way that the content of Christian faith conceptually had no substantive intellectual connection to what human reason grasps about "reality as a whole" (#35). The effectual truth of this reconfiguration was that Christian piety would gradually come to supplant Christian faith, that Christianity would less and less be seen as a faith formulated in doctrines than as a religion in which one piously believes.

If the first stage of de-Hellenization sought to rescue faith from being contaminated by putatively foreign and distorting theoretical and meta-physical formulations, the second aimed to forge a new alliance between faith and reason. This approach, which Benedict associates with the thought of Harnack, preserved the Reformers' basic prejudice against the way clas-sical Christianity and classical philosophy understood the nature and scope of reason. But where the Reformers desired to protect faith from reason,

---

[1] Compare, for example, Calvin's argument in chapter 7 of the first volume of his *Institutes of the Christian Religion* with the argument Spinoza maps out in Chaps. 13 and 14 of his *Theologico-Political Treatise.*

the proponents of the second stage of de-Hellenization sought to make faith more rational and scientific.

Accepting modern science's "self-limitation of reason" (#40), a series of nineteenth-century Christian thinkers undertook a historically critical and hence allegedly scientific study of Christian faith. In pursuit of the historical Jesus, such investigations focused on the empirically verifiable facts about the life of Jesus of Nazareth. Christian thought, it was alleged, gained scientific legitimacy only when shorn of everything that could not be documented by a critical study of the historical record. As Benedict points out, the reinterpretation of Christian faith along these lines revealed a Christ who was merely "the father of a humanitarian moral message" (#38).[2] Employing a methodology that implicitly denied Christ's divinity and the reality of man's transcendent destiny, this historically critical study of Christian faith affirmed a Christ who "put an end to worship in favour of morality" (#38). The second stage of de-Hellenization thus built upon the insistence of early modern political philosophy that practical and empirical reason should be privileged over theoretical reason, even if that insistence meant that practical reason could not actually account for the true grounds of moral and political life. That insistence fueled Hobbes's bold denial of any *summum bonum* or Kant's defense of the radical autonomy of practical reason.

Curiously, in making this argument Benedict associates, or at least draws no essential distinction between, premodern and modern science. Illustrative of this fact is that he twice, perplexingly in my judgment, associates Platonism with Cartesianism. In #40 and #43, Benedict emphasizes that both Platonic and Cartesian science necessarily presuppose the mathematical structure of matter. He does not, however, address the fact that Descartes' teaching, unlike Plato's, presupposes and explicitly issues in an emphatically non-teleological account of in-formed matter. On the question of the teleological character of nature and science, their two teachings could not be any more different. Simply put, Benedict does not draw attention to the conflict that Swift famously characterized as the essential grounds of the quarrel between the ancients and the moderns.

Currently, according to Benedict, we live in the third stage of de-Hellenization. On the basis of the modern experience of cultural pluralism, our postmodern theorists assert that Christianity's traditional understanding

---

[2] For a profound reflection on the dehumanizing effects of this position, see Flannery O'Connor's "Introduction to a Memoir of Mary Ann" in *Flannery O'Connor: Collected Works* (New York: Library of America, 1988), 822–31.

of the relationship between faith and reason is itself culturally conditioned. Classical Christianity's account of this relationship does not reveal something fundamentally true about the nature of either faith or reason, let alone their relation to each other. Rather, that relationship is accidental, a byproduct of Christianity gaining its initial cultural foothold in a particular place at a particular time.

The third stage of de-Hellenization accordingly represents a genuine flight from reason. Drawn to its logical conclusion, it requires faith and reason to be subsumed into the allegedly broader and more fundamental category of Culture. Purportedly, only then can the "simple message of the New Testament" be inculturated anew again and again (#51). Only then can Christian faith truly have intercultural meaning and produce life-sustaining "values." This stage of de-Hellenization draws the necessary conclusion from the first stage's rejection of reason and metaphysics: if what men believe truly has no discernible correlation to what reason grasps about the nature of reality, then every claim in the end must be based on a construction.

This, of course, is precisely the conclusion Max Weber drew in his famous 1919 lecture "Science as a Vocation." Drawing upon Nietzsche's diagnosis of the natural trajectory of philosophic rationalism, Weber argued that philosophy's ruthless identification of reason with rationalism has brought about what he memorably called the "disenchantment" of the world. With unprecedented successes, modern rationalism has exorcised any hidden sense of meaning or "value" in man's world. In the wake of Nietzsche's "annihilating critique" of the "last men" who naively believed they "had discovered happiness," no sober-minded, that is, rationally thinking, man could think reason can discover anything vitally true or meaningful in our world. The perpetuation of such a delusion about reasoning, according to Weber, remains the exclusive province of the churches, who, Weber was more than eager to point out, necessarily demand their own form of "intellectual sacrifice."[3]

Against this backdrop, Benedict argues that "the fundamental decisions" the early intellectual caretakers of Christianity made about the relationship between faith and reason "are part of the faith itself" (#53). Benedict repeatedly emphasizes the internal reasons why Christian faith gradually but still inevitably sought a "rapprochement" with "Greek philosophical

---

[3] Max Weber, "Science as a Vocation" in *Max Weber: Sociological Writings* (New York: Continuum, 1994), 303.

inquiry" (#29).[4] However, it would be a mistake to conclude that Benedict's primary concern here is with the essential relationship between Christian faith and Greek philosophy. This is no doubt one of his concerns, but his ultimate concern lies elsewhere. It is the prior and, in some sense, more basic relationship between Christian faith and reason. Viewed in this light, the question of faith and Greek philosophy is a secondary question. Reason and philosophy are undoubtedly related to one another. Yet we must resist the temptation to conflate the two things, to identify reason simply or too readily with philosophic reason.

This point is reflected in the lecture's title. The address is entitled "Faith, Reason and the University: Memories and Reflections," not "Faith, Philosophy and the University: Memories and Reflections." Moreover, the term *philosophy* is used sparingly in the lecture. In fact, it appears only five times, in #33, #45, #58, and twice in #60. And on two other occasions, in #39 and #61, it refers to arguments that are "seemingly" and "falsely" philosophical. By contrast, the term *reason* appears thirty-three times in the lecture. Most revealing, Benedict argues that it is the Greek understanding of reason, not simply Greek philosophy, that explains why the Church Fathers sought to forge a rapprochement between faith and reason. For both the "best" of Greek thought and Christian faith share a movement towards the *logos*. Both presuppose a conception of reason that is genuinely metaphysical in scope.

Greek thought "dared" to raise the question of Being with all of its force and in all its complexity. Benedict notes a similar raising of this question in the name God reveals to Moses in Exodus 3:14: "I am Who I am." Further still, Christianity's doctrines of the Trinity and the Incarnation necessarily made thinking about metaphysical questions unavoidable. If truth be told, there is an implicit metaphysic at work in the central doctrinal affirmations of the Christian faith. Illustrative of this fact is John's statement that in the beginning was the *Logos*. For Benedict, this scriptural claim powerfully reveals the grounds of classical Christianity's argument that reason is "consonant with the nature of faith" (#53).

Given his criticisms about the modern attempt to de-Hellenize Christianity, it is curious Benedict notes that classical Christianity carried out its own particular program of de-Hellenization. He hints at this when he remarks that Christianity forged a rapprochement not with Greek philosophy *tout court* but rather with a "critically purified Greek heritage" (#31). That Greek thought had to be critically purified is subtly associated

---

[4] See also #20.

with "Socrates' *attempt* to vanquish and transcend" the religious myths of antiquity (#20, emphasis added). Benedict here suggests that in this effort Socrates' reach exceeded his grasp. Some light is shed on this admittedly cryptic statement when we recall that Socrates' attempt took the form of his dialectical investigation into the nature of the whole. Such dialectics culminate, for Plato's and Xenophon's Socrates, not in the possession of wisdom but in the more modest love of wisdom.[5] This point is indirectly made in the very section of the sole Platonic dialogue cited in the Regensburg Lecture, the *Phaedo* (#61). In it, Plato's Socrates responds to the problem of misology with an exhortation for us to blame ourselves and not arguments, even sophistical ones, for our inability to know "the truth and knowledge of the things that *are*." This recognition, as Socrates later indicates, appears to be the ground of his so-called second sailing: Socrates now dialectically begins to examine the most reasonable, authoritative opinions about the most important things in the hope that this approach would reveal something about the nature of the whole.[6]

This reference helps explain Benedict's observation that the successful refutation of the account classical poetry gave of piety and of the gods finally required not simply Socratic philosophy but the "new understanding of God" that biblical thought brought about (#21). Benedict elaborates on this point in his *Introduction to Christianity*.[7] In that work, he points out that by siding with *logos* over myth, classical philosophy and biblical thought each sought to demythologize the world and religion. Plato's Socrates referred to this effort as the grounds of the "old quarrel between philosophy and poetry."[8] That quarrel lies at the heart of Socrates' dialectical inquiry into the city's purportedly divine laws. It was the original form of theologico-political investigation. Prior to the philosophic discovery of natural right, the good was identified with the ancestral, and the ancestral, as Aristophanes stingingly reminded Socrates in the *Clouds*, is said to have its roots in the will of the gods and the *theos nomos* they gave to man.

---

[5] See Socrates' argument about the philosopher being *the* erotic man inasmuch as he is a lover of wisdom, in Plato's *Symposium*, especially 204a–d.

[6] See Plato, *Phaedo*, trans. Eva Brann (Newburyport, Mass.: Focus, 1998), 90c–d, 95a–102a.

[7] Joseph Ratzinger, *Introduction to Christianity*, trans. J. R. Foster (New York: Herder and Herder, 1973). Subsequent references are given in parentheses in the text.

[8] Plato, *Republic*, trans. Joe Sachs (Newburyport, Mass.: Focus, 2006), 607b.

Christianity, in turn, "put itself resolutely on the side of truth and turned its back on a conception of religion satisfied to be mere outward" ceremony (97). Nor is this all, for as Christ stated, his kingdom is not of this world. The transpolitical religion he founded announced the Good News of the kingdom of God and ultimately directed man's gaze to his communion with God in eternal life. With this, Christianity made a decisive break with the pagan religions; rejecting the very notion of political theology, Christianity "disowned the misuse of the Gospel to justify a political situation" (121). In making this point, Benedict explicitly refers to the most famous and rightly controversial twentieth-century exponent of "political theology," Carl Schmitt. Schmitt interpreted Christianity to issue in a political theology that required one to act in adherence to the moral and political commands of an always unfathomable and omnipotent Divine Will. Drawing attention to Christianity's early rejection of such an understanding of "political theology," Benedict remarks that "the victory of belief in the Trinity over Monarchianism signified a victory over the political abuse of theology: the ecclesiastical belief in the Trinity shattered the politically usable molds, destroyed the potentialities of theology as a political myth" (121).[9]

But while Greek philosophy and Christianity jointly rejected this notion of political theology, their understandings of the divine still differed in important and substantive ways. Both claim that the divine is the highest being. Nevertheless, "Christian faith gave a completely new significance to this God... removing him from the purely academic realm and thus profoundly transforming him" (99). Within Christianity, divinity is no longer understood simply as the highest being, whose perfection demands it remain fixed and unchanged, knowing only itself. The "highest mode of Being" is revealed to be a Person who "includes an element of relationship" (102). The God who is triune, in other words, also reveals himself to Moses as both "I am" *and* the God of "Abraham, Isaac, and Jacob."

What is more, Christianity revealed that the "God of faith, as thought, is also love... that truth and love are originally identical" (103). There is accordingly an internal coherence to Christianity's claim that the *Logos* through whom all things were created subsequently became flesh to redeem and sanctify his creation. And there is a *reason* why Christianity, unlike Socratic rationalism, does not point to the philosopher's in-some-sense-private inquiry into the impersonal character of the whole as the truest form of human perfection. Rather, Christianity claims that man is a creature that seeks to know and seeks to be known, as well as a being

---

[9] See also Part II of Benedict's *Deus Caritas Est*.

that loves and seeks to be loved, by both other human beings and by God. "The message of the Gospel, and the Christian picture of God contained in it, corrects philosophy and lets us know that love is higher than mere thought [and that] absolute thought is a kind of love" (102). Christianity, in short, reveals that to love is truly divine. For this reason to love is natural to the creature created in God's image and likeness.

In articulating this "purified" understanding of God, Christian faith, Benedict is quick to acknowledge, clearly prods man's reason to exceed the grasp of "purely philosophical thinking" (102). By emboldening and elevating reason in this way, it consequently points to a "profound harmony" between faith and reason (#17).

One of the intriguing questions the lecture leaves us with is whether its internal logic requires the affirmation of a distinctively Christian philosophy. While the idea of a specifically Christian philosophy received its most notable and controversial defense in the last century in the thought of Etienne Gilson, the evidence for drawing this conclusion seems mixed at best. Benedict clearly does not suggest that a genuine *understanding* of Christian faith can be divorced from the act of faith. This appears to be the import of his remark about the "seemingly philosophical" character of doctrines such as the Incarnation and the Trinity (#39). At a minimum, one can say that Benedict here exhibits no pressing desire to argue that reason rightly understood inevitably and unambiguously issues in a Christian philosophy. At the same time, he does argue that when reason has the "courage to engage [its] whole breadth," it reasonably allows itself to be informed by faith (#62). Or to put it somewhat more provocatively, reason is most reasonable when it takes the form of faith seeking understanding.

I Am Your Brother Joseph: Ratzinger and the Rehabilitation of Reason

Nalin Ranasinghe

The full significance of Pope Benedict XVI's controversial address at Regensburg in September 2006 has yet to be properly appreciated. The pontiff's main theme, a stirring call for the re-Hellenization of the West, was drowned out by a nearly unanimous chorus of criticism. Ironically, Western academics were so carried away by shallow outrage on behalf of the 'Other' that they inadvertently illustrated the pope's point regarding the breakdown of speech and rationality. Their unwillingness to appreciate the deep connection between Greek Reason and Hebrew Revelation that constitutes the very basis of our intellectual tradition strongly suggests that many academics are at least dangerously unaware of, and perhaps even consciously hostile to, their own origins. This paper will focus on how Joseph Ratzinger's winged words point the way toward the recovery of a richer understanding of both reason and revelation. It is just such an intellectual and spiritual renaissance that is badly needed today.

We should first recall that this address was delivered by a former academic of notable eminence, arguably the most erudite occupant of the papacy, to an audience of former colleagues at the University of Regensburg. However, as the title of this essay suggests, the relationship between the speaker and his fellow intellectuals has not always been marked by serenity or amicability. Indeed, the story of Joseph, sold into Egyptian slavery by his brothers, provides an apt analogy. After rising to distinction in the service of the Pharaoh, Joseph, as the viceroy of Egypt, meted out rough justice to his brothers when later events placed them at his mercy. The words "I am your brother Joseph" convey more than Joseph's easy triumph over his hapless siblings. (That revelation would not take us much beyond vengeful Odysseus's dramatic appearance before his wife's suitors.) Neither do Joseph's words indicate merely a magnanimous desire to show his undeserving brothers love and mercy. The true beauty of the passage lies in Joseph's sudden, belated recollection that he is their brother-Israelite and not only a prince of Egypt. Just like Joseph and his brothers, the Church and the University must see that they stand and fall together.

The Regensburg Address acknowledged that since Greek philosophy played a necessary and indispensable role in the transmission of the glad tidings of the Christian *Logos* to the Gentile world, reason is an essential aspect of the church. The pope clearly distinguished between the ongoing exegetical activity of reason rightly understood and the stridently anti-intellectual approach of various fundamentalist Islamic and Christian sects. But even more important, he also subtly clarified the proper role of reason in a way that may help Western humanism to recover the moral and intellectual high ground from the unholy trinity of materialism, libertarianism, and positivism animating today's technological juggernaut, the hideous strength of which is threatening the integrity of human society and gravely jeopardizing the frail life-world of our planet. Benedict showed us that far from being the implacable foe of reason, science, and progress, Christianity rightly understood provides the only possible basis for the true flourishing of human civilization.

From the beginning of the address, Pope Benedict emphasizes the connections between speech, reason, and the university, making of Joseph's coat of many colors a seamless garment. He talks of "the genuine experience of *universitas*" and fondly describes a context of "lived experience" in which members of many different faculties would have "lively exchanges" despite their many different specializations because of their "basis of a single rationality with its various aspects and sharing responsibility for the right use of reason" (#4). Benedict takes especial pride in the fact that believers and non-believers alike are able to "raise the question of God through the use of reason, and to do so in the context of the tradition of the Christian faith" (#7). It is clear that he does not regard principled faith per se as an obstacle to rational dialogue between persons of different faith traditions.

Reason somehow serves as the overarching horizon under which widely varying accounts of the mysterious structure of reality can be seriously compared and fruitfully studied. We may note that light plays a similar role in Plato's *Republic*, serving as the gratuitously given permanent condition for many persons gaining and sharing knowledge of a common intelligible object. Indeed, speech itself has to obey certain fundamental preconditions or a priori categories that rule its proper functioning in the common reality.

In other words, the power of articulate human discourse presupposes the abiding existence of readily perceivable ratios of order, harmony, and regularity in the world. Since the ultimate origins of these phenomena are mysterious, there is ample room for thoughtful, reverent speculation about the various sacred accounts given concerning them.

This implicit recognition that the light of reason serves as a universal revelation is the basis for the pope's indirect condemnation of voluntaristic theology in general and radical Islam in particular. Indeed, we can observe that this very obliqueness presupposes enduring commonalities that make it possible for fruitful analogies to be drawn in many different directions. However, just as many of the great Athenian tragedies, though ostensibly about ancient Thebes or the Trojan War, were really concerned with contemporary Athens and the Peloponnesian War, it could well be the case that Islamic Fundamentalism is only a stalking horse for a far more insidious and potent threat to human rationality and dignity, one emanating from within the West itself.

Quoting the Byzantine emperor Manuel II Paleologus, the pope rejects the use of violence in the name of God in language strongly reminiscent of 1 Chronicles 11, where David refused to drink water that had been obtained for him at the cost of many lives, saying that he would not drink of the blood of brave men who had risked themselves to bring him water. The emperor, after having firmly stated that God "is not pleased by blood," goes on to say that "not acting reasonably is contrary to God's nature." This is because "Faith is born of the soul, not the body. Whoever would lead someone to faith needs the ability to speak well and reason properly, without violence and threats" (#13).

Wedding belief in God to rational speech, Pope Benedict simply but pointedly draws our attention to this essential aspect of Christianity. He does so in a way that both generously discounts the differences separating Greek Orthodoxy from Roman Catholicism and also reiterates the central role of reason and rational discourse in the Christian faith. We may infer that Christianity, a minor sect in 70 A.D., would not have survived the destruction of Jerusalem had it not been for fundamental and timeless insights into the human condition that were both preserved and fostered by its expression in the more philosophical idiom of *koine* Greek, the eponymous common tongue of the Roman Empire and Hellenized world. As a complement, the wisdom provided by Judeo-Christian Scripture gave new moral standing to the oppressed, and the example set by Christ's disciples helped the pagan world to understand the meaning of Jesus' revelations about God's love.

Neither can we forget that the way toward this relatively easy appropriation of the Christian message had been prepared by the noble example of Socrates. The dauntless old philosopher's pious deconstruction of Homeric polytheism and his enacted preference for virtue over life itself, as well as his outrageous claim that it was better to suffer evil than to inflict it, would soon become central aspects of Christian morality. "Biblical faith, in the Hellenistic period, encountered the best of Greek thought at a deep level, resulting in a mutual enrichment evident especially in the later wisdom literature" (#22).

We may now see something more of what Benedict means when he goes on to speak explicitly of "the profound harmony between what is Greek in the best sense of the word and the Biblical understanding of faith in God" (#17). After speaking of the *logos*, "a reason which is creative and capable of self-communication" (#17), he then refers to "the intrinsic necessity of a rapprochement between Biblical faith and Greek inquiry" (#19) and goes on to recognize the importance of "Socrates' attempt to vanquish and transcend myth" (#20). We may infer from this that Christianity is at best ill-served and at worst grievously mutilated, turning into a resentful and fanatically reified shadow of itself, when, under the influence of those who cry "sola scriptura," the Bible is detached from its natural ally, Greek philosophy "in the best sense of the word." While the pope provides us with a provocative schema of the three waves through which this tragedy came about, filling in the details of this account (and paying close attention to what he prudently leaves unstated) will help us to proceed with a fuller understanding of both the full magnitude of the problem and the meaning of the radical course of treatment that he prescribes for overcoming it. He does not refer to the fourth-century events by which Christianity became the official religion of the West and henceforth relied less on Greek persuasion and more on Roman power amid the widespread breakdown of order and classical learning. Nor does he mention the eleventh-century split between the Greek and Roman churches and the sordid issues surrounding the Donation of Constantine.

Benedict's account begins with the Protestant Reformation's earnest desire to hack through the overgrown jungle of scholastic philosophy and recover the pristine purity of biblical faith. "The Reformers thought they were confronted with a faith system totally conditioned by philosophy, that is to say an articulation of the faith based on an alien system of thought... faith no longer appeared as a living historical word but as one element of an overarching philosophical system" (#33). What Luther and Calvin justly denounced (and mistakenly took to be philosophy) was something very far removed from "what is Greek in the best sense of the word." Indeed, great humanists like Erasmus and More, who were aware of both the letter and spirit of the Greeks, were just as critical of those dry and legalistic clerics who valued precedents, authorities, and forgeries far more than a *logos*-animated examined life. One could imagine how Socrates himself would have dealt with the false wisdom of those descendants of Euthyphro who, while falsely believing that they were the possessors of the truth, were in reality held hostage by their perverse love of technical discourse, their unctuous respect for power, and their rabid hatred of heresy. The reformers in turn assumed that the recovered purity of scriptural literalism would make possible the establishment of God's Kingdom on Earth. They reacted with bewilderment and rage when it became clear that human nature would not conform to a narrow scriptural template. Unfortunately, the zealous and zestful correction of perceived error is not sufficient to prove that the punisher is the guardian of truth; these acts often only harden his heart and make him steadfast in his own false certainty.

One of the timeless virtues of Greek philosophy rightly understood is its power to make humans aware that certain knowledge of matters above the heavens and below the earth is beyond the powers of discursive speech. Both Plato and Jesus seemed to know that these lofty matters could be discussed only through inspired parables and analogical myths; by rudely eliminating all poetry from religion, or by regarding mythic revelations as the literal god-given truth, we gainsay our only means of access to transcendent truth.

While the reformers of the first wave of de-Hellenization earnestly believed that only the truth would set mankind free, they failed to see that parables and myths are an indispensable means both of revealing divine matters and of keeping human beings appropriately nimble-footed and humble in their disposition toward such matters. Sadly, the chronic insecurity of men like Luther with regard to the baffling question of whether they were divinely predestined for heaven or for hell coincided with a new emphasis on certain knowledge and technical mastery. Those men of science who believed that man could have certain knowledge only of what he had made himself seemed to have been dazzlingly successful in wresting Nature's secrets from her. By ensnaring Nature in their procrustean webs and grids they unfortunately found themselves able to "know" the subjects of their inquiry only as dead or mechanical objects, wholly governed by grim necessity and rigid determinism. This meant that the proofs of God's existence provided by Descartes and Spinoza were precisely and ironically what the reformers thought they had rebelled against.

Their theology, not scholasticism, was the product of "a faith system totally conditioned by philosophy, that is to say an articulation of the faith based on an alien system of thought... faith no longer appeared as a living historical Word" (#33).

Rejecting deterministic science on the one hand and held hostage by a stale precedent-bound scholasticism on the other, the church itself was entirely unprepared to deal with the new picture of the universe so dramatically conveyed to mankind by the genius of Galileo and Newton. While the deterministic power of the new science seemed to be uncannily consistent with the deepest fears of Luther and the reformers, it also made God dwindle into relative insignificance through its capacity to perform miracles and/or stupendous feats of revelation that he either could not or would not do.

Under these dire circumstances in which reason and revelation no longer seemed to have very much in common with each other, it was no wonder that religion and piety became increasingly understood in terms of otherworldliness and blind faith. Benedict brings up Kant's famous claim that "he needed to set thinking aside in order to make room for faith." With this defensive intent, Kant "anchored faith exclusively in practical reason, denying it access to reality as a whole" (#35). The German philosopher's heroic but ultimately unsuccessful efforts to reconcile Newtonian necessity and moral freedom are also reflected in his somewhat schizophrenic claim that it is more important for man to *deserve* happiness than to *be* happy. This stark and striking distinction between virtue and happiness—a disjunction that reduces once-virile Machiavellian *virtù* to mean something like chastity or self-denial before the infinite temptations of the world, the flesh, and the devil—is all but inevitable once science seems to be the proud possessor of the art of happiness. Furthermore, under the continued tutelage of Machiavelli, it seemed that men had to learn "how to be bad" in order better to enjoy this promised happiness.

At this point the second wave of de-Hellenization took place. Faced with the increased impotence of the church in society and its strong tendency to ally itself with forces of reaction and misanthropy, enlightened men of reason drew a sharp distinction between Jesus and the church and proclaimed that the moral teachings of the former had nothing in common with the stultified doctrines and meaningless rituals of established religion. Having triumphantly slipped the repressive bonds of otherworldly religion, these men of goodwill now tried to do what the institutional church both could not do and would not allow: they set out to realize the Kingdom of Heaven on Earth. Marked by all the attributes of apocalyptic Gnosticism, this enterprise was obviously heartened by the massive triumphs, both rhetorical and intellectual, that the scientific Enlightenment had gained over what Hobbes famously called the Kingdom of Darkness. It was only a matter of time before science and technology would be able radically to transform the hitherto miserable lives of those Jesus had blessed but had been unable to liberate: the poor, the oppressed, and the handicapped.

Unlike its predecessor, which was profoundly antiphilosophic and was mostly waged by disillusioned clerics, this second wave of de-Hellenization was undertaken in the name of philosophy, albeit of a novel, non-Hellenic variety. When the pope refers to this phenomenon as "Platonism," he means by this "a synthesis between Platonism (Cartesianism) and empiricism, a synthesis confirmed by the success of technology" (#40). What is Platonic about this Cartesian project is its presupposition of the "mathematical structure of matter" and its "intrinsic rationality" (#41). The deeper significance of this project, which clearly justifies Benedict calling it Platonism rather than Cartesianism, is its utopian quality—a quality that finds its origin in Plato's most famous, or notorious, work: the *Republic* has been the unacknowledged template of the failed modern enterprise.

The twentieth century saw the culmination of half a millennium of modernism, marked by various well-intentioned and/or bloody-minded attempts to emulate the *Republic* literally and impose a post-theological Heaven on Earth by combining materialistic metaphysics, draconian technology, and social engineering. All of these Promethean endeavors ended in abject failure. They killed over a hundred million human beings, ruined the lives of several billions more, and left most of us feeling deeply suspicious of all attempts to bring about revolutionary transformations of the human condition. Today the era of the *Republic* is over, and the overdetermined space of totalitarianism seems to have been abolished. Entertainment has replaced both edification and education as the primary sense of the meaning of life. No longer believing that the human being's psychic and intellectual powers could be directed toward the attainment of heaven or the recovery of paradise on earth, many postmodern intellectuals are content to cannibalize their higher faculties and place them at the disposal of base or banal passions.

While the *Republic*, if read properly, teaches that a virtuous political regime may be established only in the soul and not in the city, it does not take us much beyond this point. The literal enactment of the *Republic* failed because science and technology could not reform human nature; post-Enlightenment human beings could not reenter the Garden of Eden as happy contented animals because the human soul perversely refused to wither away. Today, in the West, while the state may well be said to have been superseded by market forces, the infinite desires of the soul aroused by the seductions of modernity rage on unabated amid the ashes of the modern project itself. It is here that we feel the third wave of de-Hellenization, and it is at this point that the re-Hellenization of civilization must begin.

Although Benedict is very terse here, for reasons that may have to do with the failed ecumenism of his predecessors, we may decipher the main threads of his argument. The third wavers, says the pope, claim that "the synthesis with Hellenism achieved in the early Church was an initial inculturation which ought not to be binding on other cultures. The latter are said to have the right to return to the simple message of the New Testament prior to that inculturation...to inculturate it anew in their own particular milieux" (#51). The implication is that at this final stage of de-Hellenization, the church, after previously having become separated from both philosophy and science, now must complete this sorry saga by tossing out its own historical origins. Since Platonism is assumed by postmodernism to be identical with the Cartesianism of the modern project, Plato is ritually condemned for the sins of his illicitly cloned progeny. We must burn our conceptual rainbow-bridges, the third wavers insist, and plunge into the pure flux of becoming. However, as the sea of faith recedes, only the sweet sentiment of solidarity with the oppressed gives spiritual meaning to the life of the *bien pensant*. Gushingly impotent expressions of the infinite guilt of the West towards the 'Other' replace honest acknowledgment of cultural differences; the integrity of Christianity itself is undermined by a guilt-sodden sentimentality that all too often surpasses understanding, evades responsibility, and oozes *ressentiment*. Even today, personal charisma and nihilistic humanitarianism are often used to generate moral responses to calamities that dogma and piety cannot cope with.

While it is indeed true that the grand experiment of modernity had disastrous results, the pope is asking us whether Reason, Christianity, and the West are all radically discredited by this debacle. By insisting that God is not pleased by coercive conversion and claiming that faith is born of the soul through reason and persuasion, Benedict is reiterating the rational integrity and freedom of that very indigestible spiritual substance that caused the downfall of the various modernist utopias: the human soul, the discovery of which was the very origin of Hellenism. He also sharply distinguishes between the coercive methods of instrumental reason and the *logos* that rightly persuades the human soul. Quoting Plato's *Phaedo*, the pope warns us against misology, a frustration with the abuse of reason that leads to an aversion of reason itself (#61). As this misology leads the stubborn to turn to biblical literalism, Marian devotion, and Ultramontane doctrine, the tender-hearted are consumed by nihilistic humanitarianism.

Ironically, even as postmodern academics and theologians reject and revile reason, their ritual denunciations are almost irrelevant; instrumental reason is more powerful than ever in postmodernity. Technology is so ubiquitous and invisible today that its processes are no longer intelligible to even the most educated and well-informed individuals. It is this dehumanizing species of reason that seems to be the true target of the pope's address. Otherwise, we cannot reconcile his critical account of de-Hellenization and his defense of reason with the crass realities of the technological world in which we live. Differently put, while the excesses of high modernity caused much academic and clerical revulsion against reason, these protests don't matter much in our postmodern cave where the lives and interactions of even its harshest critics are silently held together by technology.

The question then is whether the West can possibly regain its spiritual and intellectual integrity by recovering its Hellenic roots. While clearly this can occur only through reason and *logos* being rightly understood, it remains to be seen whether this synthesis can persuade our jaded desires and lazy bodies. In other words, because reason rightly understood can act only by the genuine persuasion of the soul, it could be the case that our disordered psychic regimes are unmoved by reason's authority. But since Pope Benedict has affirmed that God acts on the human soul through the *logos*, "a reason which is creative and capable of self-communication" (#17), such a state of affairs would effectively mean that God is dead to technological man. Indeed, the reflexive vilification and simple incomprehension that greeted the Regensburg address may provide chilling confirmation of this dire condition. Or we could return to our Hellenic roots and argue, using the Myth of the Cave as our proof-text, that it is always possible to use philosophical dialectic to persuade a soul mired in artificial reality to get rightly acquainted with reality and rule its desires through self-knowledge and rational persuasion.

Everything hinges on whether technology has truly "invented the art of happiness," as Nietzsche put it. If so, and the fallen soul is ruled by violations of its own order, then Benedict is wrong. We are indeed in the age of the Last Man, and God is dead. Conversely, if the happiness that is offered in the postmodern cave turns out to be false, we may be more hopeful about the fate of mankind. The soul's stubborn refusal to wither away before totalitarianism was the death-knell of modernity. Could this restlessness of the human heart also defeat the more insidious hedonistic self-violence of postmodernity and lead the West to be reborn with renewed self-knowledge?

Today's technology of happiness promises mankind thoughtlessness, silence, separation, and distraction. It flies in the face of all that is represented by the *logos*: reason, speech, community, and presence-in-the-world. The pope warns that if we allow technology to define what is meaningful and rational, then moral judgments will be seen as subjective epiphenomena. Furthermore "ethics and religion lose their power to create a community" (#49). Their spokespersons then become shrill, impotent, irresponsible protesters against the crass *ananke*-like tyranny of supply and demand. If, on the other contrary, we refuse to banish the School of Hellas from Christendom, there are far more virile voices on our side to defend the integrity of the human soul. The quarrel between Athens and Jerusalem, both victims of an earlier globalization, is proved false and should not be allowed to exclude those pagan voices and minds that played an essential role in the building of civilization. Greek *eros* and poetry must not be exiled by censorious Roman legalism, a force with rather too close an affinity to power dynamics, property rights, and today's materialism. We should rather follow the example of the exiled Dante (who was after all following the example of the church fathers) and smuggle these pagan muses back into our tradition.

These three forces of fundamentalism, technology, and nihilistic humanitarianism all continue to exist as ravaging monsters spawned by the Roman Church's inability to come to terms with the Greek aspects of its origins. Each force began as a response to a genuine crisis within the church before then becoming a massive problem in its own right. But these issues can be corrected only when Christianity's Greek roots are recovered and not jettisoned, as the nihilistic humanitarians would have us do today. Benedict reminds us that "The New Testament was written in Greek and bears the imprint of the Greek Spirit" (#52). This retrieval of Hellenism can take place only through *logos*-bearing speech; it cannot occur through divine dispensation, magisterial diktat, or curial jargon. The ugly silence of the cave of technology must be broken by rational dialogic speech. This word is best heard in the sanctuary of an academic setting, at universities dedicated to recovering the unity of truth and knowledge. There, true happiness must be seen to issue from intellectual generosity and spiritual communion. The role of the university is thus to display this great truth to humanity.

When the pope celebrated the vitality of academic life at Regensburg, he was doing far more than indulging in septuagenarian nostalgia; he was describing a place where all parties could enter into honest respectful dialogue with the intent of finding the truth, living the good life, and recovering a common love of the world. Such an academic ethos is the only possible setting in which the church can become honestly reacquainted with her Hellenic roots; legalistic curial bureaucrats and self-appointed guardians of fideism are usually too authoritarian, inflexible, or adversarial for the delicate process of negotiating with free-spirited humanists and recovering a *logos* of the original elements of the Christian tradition. This urgently needed conversation should not be hamstrung by a desire for short-term polemical advantage or silenced by the dead weight of past precedent. By setting a place at the high table for his brother academicians, Joseph Ratzinger suggests that intellectual probity and thoughtful religiosity belong together at all institutions of higher learning dedicated to recovering the splendor and unity of truth.

In today's universities crass bureaucratic necessity and irresponsible academic anarchism are typically in constant conflict. Consequently there is minimal concern shown toward either the discovery of truth or its cultivation. Because of an emphasis on jargon, technique, and specialization, knowledge is no longer synthesized in the human mind; there are very few academics with a broadly informed understanding of how the various areas of human knowledge hang together. Many postmodern humanists seem to be trying to pass a sort of inverted Turing test, one that requires their work to be as pseudo-scientific as possible, even though their paradigms conform only to the obsolete categories of nineteenth-century positivism. Believing that "only the kind of certainty resulting from the interplay of mathematical and empirical elements can be considered scientific," they are certain that the human sciences must "attempt to conform themselves to this canon of scientificity" (#45).

Conversely, and even more strikingly, many believing intellectuals practice a flat-footed fideism and maintain the strictest separation between their "double truths" of unreflective faith and instrumental thought. But though such a stoic stance is quite consistent with Roman legalism, making it quite easy for the same person to praise God and service Mammon, still "God does not become more divine when we push him away from us in a sheer, impenetrable voluntarism" (#27). It does not suffice to aver resolutely that Jonah was swallowed by a whale; this only makes us more prone to obey power mindlessly and less likely to live by the teachings of "the truly divine God…who has revealed himself as *logos* and, as *logos*, has acted and continues to act lovingly on our behalf" (#27). Blindly praising God's irrational will and unlimited power confirms every charge of irresponsibility leveled against religion by fundamentalism's deadly adversary, the technological juggernaut that corrupts the university and causes the state to wither away. By discrediting reason and giving rise to antirational humanitarian nihilism, this deadly struggle between angry fundamentalism and violent technology suggests that happiness is incompatible with the burden of the *logos* and justifies the spawning of the Last Man.

The pope challenges the university to reverse this dismal trend and set both church and society on a nobler path. He looks forward to a scientific spirit that by "broadening our concept of reason and its application" (#56) may embody "the will to be obedient to the truth," an attitude essential to the Christian spirit (#55). This reversal can happen only if "reason and faith come together in a new way," one that will "overcome the self-imposed limitation of reason to the empirically falsifiable" and "once more disclose its vast horizons" (#56). This coming together must also combine both senses of the word *logos,* as reason and speech respectively, in contrast to fundamentalism, which employs speech against reason; technology, which is reified reason without speech; and nihilistic humanitarianism, which uses speech and finds reasons to follow the bleak advice of Job's wife: it would "curse God and die."

In Benedict's vision, conversely, the re-Hellenized university must be a place where cultivated human beings discover and celebrate the beauty and bounty of the created universe, where they can reconnect with the great cosmic mysteries that are being discovered every day by pure scientists. In keeping with the spirit of Attic tragedy, re-Hellenized scholars will confront the darkest texts and issues of bygone times with honesty and responsibility; legalistic literalism and blind loyalty to the past must not be allowed to poison the future. As with Joseph and his brothers, old mistakes must be admitted to, atoned for, and forgiven. The truth must out.

By his stirring account of the divine *Logos* and his lively vindication of the power of human rationality as its bearer and interlocutor, Joseph Ratzinger, Pope Benedict XVI, has reaffirmed the dignity of the human person. Rejecting both the "Death of Man" proclaimed by postmodernism and the misanthropic piety of fideism, he challenges the university to be true to its *logos*-bearing essence and come to the defense of the church and the world. We cannot let this rare opportunity slip. A new Pharaoh "who has not heard not of Joseph" could well be the precursor of a terrible new dark age made more sinister by the lights of perverted science.

God Is Great or God Is Good
(Let Us Thank Him for Our Mood)

Bruce Fingerhut

When Pope Benedict gave his magisterial Regensburg Lecture on September 12, 2006, the mass media emphasized only one part of one paragraph in the address, a quotation the pope took from a fourteenth-century Byzantine emperor—a quotation that enflamed Muslims throughout the world, virtually none of whom had read it. Demonstrations, riots, even a murder of a nun and her bodyguard followed. Apologies were universally demanded of the pope, and there were calls for his assassination. Put succinctly, the argument was "You insult us by calling us violent. So death to you." Sadly, these were the progeny of people who reintroduced Aristotelian logic to the West.

The question in that regard is, "Is it legitimate to spread the faith through the sword?" The pope's answer, the answer of Christendom for a millennium at least, is no. "God," said the emperor, "is not pleased by blood." The faith must be embraced by an unforced will and communicated through a free reason. God created the world by his word, by his *logos*, to use the Greek term. This is seen explicitly both in the creation story in Genesis, in which he creates the world out of nothing but his speech, and in the opening of St. John's Gospel, in which he is equated with the Word. Moreover, the main work God put upon man in paradise was to name things.

Further, in addition to being an instrument of creation, the word is also a communication. When God gives his human creations his word, in all senses of *word*, they are created in his image; that is, they are imbued with *ratio*, the rational faculty that allows them to understand, to comprehend, and to judge. They are an image and imitation of their Creator.

But the theme of the current rise of inexorable religious hatred in the Muslim world was almost ancillary in the pope's argument, a result of the absence of commonality in reason, what he called "dehellenization" when it came to Christianity, especially as it applies in the original bedrock of Christianity, Europe. But let me take the more obvious case of Islam first, a case centering on the notions of will and its main philosophic theory, voluntarism.

For the Muslim, God is absolutely transcendent. His will is not bound up with any of our categories, even that of rationality. (The Muslim theologian Ibn Hazm even went so far as to say that God is not bound even by his own word and that nothing would oblige him to reveal the truth to us.) And while it is true that the Old Testament has snippets of voluntarist actions attributed to God, the central foundations of Christianity were nonvoluntarist. God has limited himself and abides by his self-imposed limits. Moreover, he is predictable. Jesus Christ, says the writer of Hebrews, "is the same yesterday, today, and for ever." And Jesus is quoted in the three synoptic Gospels as promising, "Heaven and earth shall pass away, but my words will not pass away." He is therefore knowable, even though some may say he is known only negatively, that is, by what he is not. He communicates to us and hears us because the means of communication between us, rationality and word, are held in common by us.

Allah, on the other hand, because he is not bound by categories, remains inscrutable. Assertions made on his behalf cannot help portraying him as a willful and moody god.

But let us be fair. Is the situation in Islam now that much different from the way it was in the ninth or tenth centuries? The religion was born of the sword. And it has the further difficulty of having its holy book not simply written under divine inspiration by mortals, as in the case of the Scriptures in Judaism and Christianity, but dictated by Allah himself, at a specific time to a specific person in a specific language. The words themselves are holy. Interpretation is thus become a dangerous occupation because it seeks to dethrone the holy, in a sense to replace it with human ideas, or ideas on a human scale. The differences that obtain among Islamic sects today come from power politics and the relationship between wealth and technology in large measure—wealth that was gained through the happenstance of raising tents over the largest cache of oil in the world. The only people with the power to take it from them are bound by a distinctly non-Islamic law and equity not to do so.

My thesis is that the pope's critique was *principally* not of the voluntarist aspects of Islam but of those very aspects in Reformation Christianity that, in introducing a corrective to the understanding of Christianity, over-corrected to such an extent that the God they wished to be more accessible became instead more distant. The Reformation's argument was that philosophy got in the way of scriptural formulations. The Reformers wanted a faith unconditioned by philosophy. The result was subsumed under the rubric "sola scriptura." But as James V. Schall made clear in *The Regensburg Lecture*, Scripture is not just read or absorbed by osmosis; it must be understood, and the mind must acknowledge real things, not only words, as the starting point and the source of new knowledge. Lacking this ability, a man will not be saved by reading Scripture. Throwing out metaphysics because of its lineage left the faith standing alone, "indifferent to the presuppositions that were contained in the minds of those who heard it."

All order and disorder, implies the pope, begin in the mind, where the real battles are. The casting out of metaphysics does not mean that the faith shines through untarnished; the place of the rejected first principles supplied by metaphysics must be filled with other first principles, and sooner or later someone will come forth to confront us on them. Kant did so when he drew the conclusion that to protect the faith, not only must we set aside metaphysics, but, as the pope put it, we "needed to set thinking aside in order to make room for faith" (#35). Once thinking and faith became wholly unrelated, faith was downgraded as illegitimate in the academy and the public square, since both its origin and execution were seen as private. In the Catholic understanding, formulated as "*credo ut intelligam*" ("I believe that I may understand"), faith is not a rival or alternative to reason. With the Reformers' assertion of "sola fides," a formula that faith alone is sufficient for man to know how to live, the privacy of scriptural interpretation was made more radical. If "sola scriptura" makes every man his own priest, it is hard to see in "sola fides" how any man escapes being his own god, since such a man can know only himself with surety and will therefore have a different understanding of reality from his fellow men. The intimacy the Reformers sought with God and his Word ended with a world in which each man was alienated from all others *and* from God.

The pope calls this process "dehellenization," not only because it has taken philosophy away from the faith, but because it has consigned reason to materialist actions only. It has managed, in separating faith and understanding, to diminish both. It limits faith to private introspections and reason to quantitative materialist interplay. The diminishment of faith and reason, of course, has meant the diminishment of man.

The result of this "dehellenization" has been the so-called post-Christian West. When commentators mention this term, more often than not, they are referring to the emergence of the spirit of the West (with the prominent and bemoaned exception of the United States) from the dark ages of myth and cult into the bright blue (though unfortunately greenhouse-gas-filled) sky of postmodernity, free from annoying behavioral prescriptions, into the marvelous light promised by the Enlightenment's vision of reason.

But it is precisely the opposite of true reason that has been the lot of Europe. Reason may seem to be more openly accepted, but that is only because it has been applied to such a diminished part of the life of man. In fact, in the core of man's being, *none* of the most important questions can be addressed by this diminished reason.

In the meantime, the arguments from the "dehellenists" (for want of a better term) are puerile at best. Read Richard Dawkins, read Christopher Hitchens, who write with subtlety and perception in their own field. When it comes to faith and God, however, their writing becomes mere rant, spewing hatred, not argument; they are indignant that there are troglodytes left whose backward ways demand an answer. But the answer these men give has nothing to do with reason, nothing to do with argument. Instead of writing something because they understand how a phenomenon came to be and exists (as they would in their own fields), they are writing precisely because they *don't* understand it, find it impossible to understand, and their lack of understanding the thoughts and beliefs of others leads them, not to argument, but to frustration and hatred. It makes for pretty thin gruel, best-seller gruel though it be.

One is hard-pressed to find a first-rate argument for atheism in the past hundred and fifty years. Even Nietzsche, subtle and brilliant though he was, never addressed Christianity on its own basis because he thought he was part of a post-metaphysical world. The writer who, in my mind, really addressed the atheist question head on and made the best argument for it was Dostoevsky, for he knew the will to power better than Nietzsche and could portray a weakened god, though his weakness was self-imposed, better than Zarathustra. The chaos he predicted in the heart of Ivan Karamazov came about soon after his own death, which chaos followed the easy grace and hedonism so perceptively put into the personality of Dmitri. His Grand Inquisitor knew the result of tearing asunder reason and revelation. Indeed, it is now everywhere to be seen: Europe unwilling to stand up to barbarism, defenseless before the new Mongols.

In such an undefended battlefield, it would seem that Islam, always more concerned with submission to God than with knowing Him, has the advantage. "God is great," they say. *Allahu akbar.* Of course, that is likely to be the last words you hear before they slit your throat. Good and evil are not to be applied to the category-less God, and thus their exclamation of God's power is a call to arms rather than a song of praise.

The question that confronts us today concerns whether the Christian understanding that God is primarily good, a category that requires both our reason and our faith to understand and act upon it, can withstand the onslaught of a world in which faith and reason are mutually exclusive—a world we see rapidly appearing before our eyes. In such a world, either God is great *or* God is good.

Math, Modernity, and the Stubbornness of Literature

Glenn Arbery

Some years ago, when my family lived in a huge old house in New Hampshire, we used to accommodate students who needed a place to stay in the summer. They helped with the yard work and paid no rent, but the spare room to which we consigned these unfortunates was up on the third floor in the back of the house, just under the roof. They could stand up if they stayed under the rectangle of ceiling from the door over to the back window, but the room sloped down sharply on both sides. One wit among them immediately named it "the Raskolnikov room." We laughed—and hid our ax.

Readers of Dostoevsky's *Crime and Punishment* usually remember, if they forget almost everything else but the murders, the oppressive sense of Raskolnikov's little yellow room high up the stairs, "more like a cupboard than a place to live in" (1),[1] which he later calls a "wretched little hole" where he "lurked in a corner like a spider" (352) Any mention of that room summons up the claustrophobia, if not arachnophobia, associated with inhuman theories. When I read Pope Benedict's remarks about "the modern self-limitation of reason" in his Regensburg Lecture, I think of that room in St. Petersburg, the new capital of Russia founded by Peter the Great's brutal fiat. Dostoevsky once called it "the most artificial city in the world."[2]

---

[1] Feodor Dostoevsky, *Crime and Punishment*, trans. Jessie Coulson, ed. George Gibian, 3rd ed. (New York: Norton, 1989). Subsequent references are given in parentheses in the text.

[2] When Peter the Great founded it in 1703 at the mouth of the Neva and drained the marshlands using forced labor, "There was no housing, no food, no tools for them," according to Solomon Volkov in *St. Petersburg: A Cultural History* (New York: Free Press, 1997). "They transported excavated dirt in

Can a novel published in 1865 have anything important to say about the issues that the Pope raises in his lecture? In a key passage toward the end, Benedict writes, "Modern scientific reason quite simply has to accept the rational structure of matter and the correspondence between our spirit and the prevailing rational structures of nature as a given, on which its methodology has to be based. Yet the question why this has to be so is a real question, and one which has to be remanded by the natural sciences to other modes and planes of thought—to philosophy and theology" (#59–#60). He says nothing about literature, and the reasons seem obvious. In the first place, he is addressing the science faculty. Why should a novel have anything foundational to say about "the correspondence between our spirit and the prevailing rational structures of nature"? Nevertheless, it would not sound absurd to me if Pope Benedict had told the faculty of science at Regensburg to read Dostoevsky and to take modern literature very seriously indeed. As the novelist Milan Kundera writes, literature has a unique place in modernity: "Once elevated by Descartes to 'master and proprietor of nature,' man has now become a mere thing to the forces (of technology, of politics, of history) that bypass him, surpass him, possess him. To those forces, man's concrete being, his 'world of life'...has neither value nor interest: it is eclipsed, forgotten from the start."[3] Kundera argues that literature restores this "world of life." In the great writers, literature embodies an analogical way of thinking that never bypasses man's concrete being, and by refusing to forget the "world of life," it holds open the most serious questions that allow what Benedict calls "the whole breadth of reason."

The poet looks at the flow of human actions, finds discrete patterns in them, and makes them knowable. An interior movement of spirit over time, involving change in its very nature, takes on a distinct shape that becomes visible in the poetic work. Raskolnikov's name becomes synonymous not just with what he thinks but with what he does and how it affects other people in the "world of life." In revealing that action, the novel

---

their clothing.... How many died of starvation, disease, and exhaustion? Probably hundreds of thousands. Peter did not care, so no one kept track." Peter wanted it to embody Enlightenment ideas and bring Russia into Europe, for which reason he moved the capital from Moscow, splitting his new "enlightened" state from old Mother Russia. Raskolnikov's very name derives from the word for schism or split.

[3] Milan Kundera, *The Art of the Novel*, trans. Linda Asher (New York: Grove, 1988), 4.

opens the closed system of his ideas to the corrections of analogous actions in the lives of people around him, and in doing so, it raises the question of the correspondence between self-certain rationality and the larger order that contains it. If Dostoevsky had made Raskolnikov more general, less salient in his particularity, his story would be less analogous to that of other particular characters, whether it is Achilles' claim on extraordinary honor, the withdrawal of Thoreau to his cabin at Walden Pond, or the decision of a suicide bomber to blow himself up in a crowd. What I want to do, then, is to think about the action and themes of Dostoevsky's novel to show how it explores the constriction of reason that Benedict raises as a central modern problem.

Why this novel? Because Raskolnikov embodies the second phase of de-Hellenization in modern thought that the Pope discusses, especially the alienation from the common experience of a community, "the subjective 'conscience' [that] becomes the sole arbiter of what is ethical" (#48). Benedict's primary concern with subjective conscience lies in matters of religion, and he means people who decide matters for themselves without regard for the teachings of the church. But Dostoevsky exposes this subjectivity in its still darker nature. Perhaps more unexpectedly, he also addresses the modern bearing toward what Benedict calls "the mathematical structure of matter, its intrinsic rationality" (#41) and at the same time "nature's capacity to be exploited for our purposes" (#42). Subjectivity and mathematics have a strange kinship that Dostoevsky explores in the main action of *Crime and Punishment*.

The basic outlines of the story are simple. A young man from a good family falls under the influence of modern ideas and murders an old pawnbroker to prove his theory. Originally free from suspicion, he incriminates himself in several key episodes with the police and then attracts the scrutiny of the examining magistrate, a peculiar Socratic trickster named Porfiry Petrovich, before finally confessing to the crime at the end of the novel. Even before this legal confession, he has confessed privately to a very religious young prostitute named Sofya or Sonya who reads him the story of Lazarus's resurrection, urges him to kiss the earth and declare his guilt, dedicates herself to him, and eventually accompanies him to Siberia, where he at last undergoes the experience of conversion.

Raskolnikov's nature is to be spirited and generous. He gives the last money he has to the family of Sonya's father, Marmeladov, a hopeless drunk; he protects a young girl from a wealthy lecher on the street; heconfronts his sister's rich fiancé for insulting her, despite the fact that the man offers him employment that would raise him from poverty.

High-minded, drawn to the beautiful action, he has nevertheless fallen under the sway of an idea whose symbol is his room: a closed space, cut off from any community, visited only through determined charity, and harboring demonic reveries far removed from the more expansive realms of reason. Rather than being a place apart, however, like the shelter of Achilles after his withdrawal from battle or Thoreau's cabin, this room brings the malignant nature of St. Petersburg to a single point of focus. Raskolnikov's actions have their source in the subjectivity that his room represents. He later tells Sonya, "low ceilings and cramped rooms crush the mind and the spirit.... Oh, how I hated that hole. But all the same I would not leave it. I deliberately stayed in it!" (352).

What are the roots of this subjectivity? In an essay called "The Age of the World Picture," Martin Heidegger writes, "Through Descartes, realism is first put in the position of having to prove the reality of the outer world, of having to save that which is as such."[4] With Descartes, there are two kinds of certainty: first, that of the subject, the one who says, "*cogito ergo sum*," and second, that of the truths that can be proved objectively and represented to the mind. With Descartes comes a fundamental shift, says Heidegger: "The superiority of a subject (as a ground lying at the foundation)...arises out of the claim of man to a...self-supported, unshakable foundation of truth, in the sense of certainty" (148). In other words, the clear and distinct objective ideas of scientific truth, subject to verification and falsification, displace faith in God and establish man as the preeminent ground of truth. "Why and how does this claim acquire its decisive authority?" Heidegger asks. His answer has a great deal to say about the movement of soul in Raskolnikov, which recapitulates the movement of man in modernity. "The claim," writes Heidegger, "originates in that emancipation of man in which he frees himself from obligation to Christian revelational truth and Christian doctrine to a legislating *for* himself that takes its stand *upon* itself. Through this liberation, the essence of freedom, i.e., being bound by something obligatory, is posited anew. But because, in keeping with this freedom, self-liberating man himself posits what is obligatory, the latter can henceforth be variously defined" (148, emphasis added). Man, that is, can make the law for himself, based on what he can prove objectively. At the heart of Raskolnikov's quest for certainty is *his capacity as a subject* to be the absolute source of laws for himself and others. Early in the novel, he says to himself, "Grant that there is no element of doubt in all those

---

[4] In Martin Heidegger, *The Question Concerning Technology And Other Essays*, trans. William Lovitt (New York: Harper Torchbooks, 1982), 139. Subsequent references are given in parentheses in the text.

calculations of mine, grant that all the conclusions I have come to during the past month are as clear as daylight, as *straightforward as arithmetic*, all the same I shall never summon up enough resolution to do it" (51, emphasis added). Can he be an *origin*, or must he simply follow the laws of others? The question crushes him, and his desire for self-liberation takes on the form of an obsession with the old pawnbroker, Alëna Ivanovna, known to all the students.

In this one respect, Raskolnikov inhabits not the real world of other people but a theory of the world, a system, that is more or less mathematical in nature and mathematical in a modern, Cartesian sense. His reference to arithmetic would strike us as a throwaway, except that his friend Razumikhin describes his own relations to Raskolnikov's landlady as "more complicated than any of [Raskolnikov's] algebraic formulas could ever be" (105). It is a telling remark, because it implies that in the past, Raskolnikov has used mathematical formulas in describing human things, and Razumikhin (whose name comes from *razum*, reason or good sense) is joking that his relationship with the landlady is too emotionally convoluted for Raskolnikov's algebra to handle. In the *Nicomachean Ethics*, Aristotle points out that "it belongs to an educated person to look for just so much precision in each kind of discourse as the nature of the thing one is concerned with admits," and he explicitly distinguishes human action from geometry. But one of the marks of modernity has been the attempt to achieve mathematical precision in the human sciences, as the pope indicates. Benedict argues that the modern presupposition about the mathematical structure of reality and the concomitant belief that nature can be exploited for our purposes lead to two principles: "First, only the kind of certainty resulting from the interplay of mathematical and empirical elements can be considered scientific....A second point, which is important for our reflections, is that by its very nature this method excludes the question of God, making it appear an unscientific or pre-scientific question" (#45–#46). Under the first point, he argues that such human sciences as "history, psychology, sociology and philosophy, attempt to conform themselves to this canon of scientificity" (#45). Raskolnikov seems to have fallen prey to some version of this thought.

The ideas current around him in the novel come from English utilitarian and positivist thinking. Early in the book, for example, a character explains "that in this age, the sentiment of compassion is actually prohibited by science....[T]hat is how they order things in England, where they have political economy" (11). In Russia, people like his sister's self-important fiancé Luzhin embrace the idea that making money and keeping it for oneself, not trying to help one's neighbors, works better for everybody. "Carry [that] to its logical conclusion," Raskolnikov tells Luzhin, "and it emerges that you can cut people's throats" (129). The stages leading up to his murder of the old pawnbroker follow out the economic arithmetic of selfishness but with additions that Luzhin would be helpless to imagine. At the beginning of the novel, an idea has already trapped Raskolnikov. He finds himself unable to fight its murderous logic, and the reader, without knowing yet exactly what the idea is, watches him act under its compulsion and kill the old pawnbroker, then murder her simple-minded sister who happens to return before he leaves the apartment.

Dostoevsky takes his time revealing the details of his character's thought. Several days after the murders, the theory first emerges explicitly in a conversation between Raskolnikov, Razumikhin, and the examining magistrate Porfiry Petrovich. Razumikhin has been passionately denouncing utopian schemes based on science: "nature is not taken into account, nature is banished, nature is not supposed to exist!...[A] social system, devised by some mathematician's brain, will instantly reorganize humanity, make it righteous and innocent in a flash, with greater speed than any living process, and without the aid of living historical development!... [T]hey do not like the living process of life: they have no use for the *living soul*" (219). Interrupting Razumikhin, Porfiry Petrovich surprises Raskolnikov by bringing up an article called "Concerning Crime" that Raskolnikov had written for a magazine. He did not realize it had been published.

His theory does not call for utopian social reorganization, as though everyone could be made equal. Instead, it concentrates on the great individual, the "extraordinary man," whose very superiority to others makes real innovation possible. In his theory, the extraordinary man has the right "to permit his conscience to overstep certain obstacles, but only in the event that his ideas (which may sometimes be salutary for all mankind) require it for their fulfillment." For example, "if the discoveries of...Newton, by some combination of circumstances, could not have become known to the world in any other way than by sacrificing the lives of one, or ten, or a hundred or more people...Newton would have had the right, or might even have been under an obligation...to *remove* those ten or a hundred people, so that his discoveries might be revealed to all mankind" (220).[5] All the

---

[5] It's ironic that Newton did not publish his great work in mathematics for over twenty years after he finished it, and he had to be talked into publishing his calculus by his friends. See James Gleick, *Isaac Newton,* (New York: Pantheon, 2003).

great founders—he mentions Lycurgus, Solon, Mahomet, and Napoleon—
were transgressors, he says. (Machiavelli makes a related point in Chapter
VI of *The Prince.*) Why Newton, though, the great mathematician? And
how does a theoretical obligation on Newton's part turn into Raskolnikov's
actual deed?

Porfiry draws him out, playing on his pride, as Socrates does his own
arrogant, young interlocutors, and the inferences become increasingly
clear. If the extraordinary man has to be capable of transgression, then
there must be some exact moment, one transgression, which first opens
reality to him in a new way. There must be one first deed by which he steps
over from the conventional world into a new one, one act that introduces
the truth that he calls his "New Word," with echoes of the beginning of the
Gospel of John. What this moment will be remains indeterminate, and until
opportunity supplies it, he himself remains the unknown, the x, in his own
formulation. The genius of Dostoevsky lies in showing that Raskolnikov's
waiting for this opportunity transforms his experience into an uncanny,
superstitious half-attendance on what happens around him, a dark version
of attention to providence.

Two things in Raskolnikov's thought are distinctively modern. One is
the *theorizing* of transgression, an implicit polemic against Christian moral
restraint whose roots lie in Machiavelli. "Fortune is a woman," writes
Machiavelli, "and it is necessary, if one wants to hold her down, to beat her
and strike her down."[6] The other is modern in a mathematical sense that
differs from the ancient one, as Jacob Klein argues in *Greek Mathematical Thought and the Origins of Algebra.*[7] Modern algebra no longer has
continuous specific reference to the particulars of the natural world. It is no
longer rooted in a conversation with real things.

It seems paradoxical that modern mathematics, which underlies the very
possibility of modern physics and seems to have everything to do with the
reign of technology, should be *less* related to the real world of things, say,
than Euclidean geometry with its spaceless points and pristine planes. But
the emphasis in modern mathematics, starting with algebra, is on *method*,
employing such concepts as "general magnitude," number in the abstract.

---

[6] Niccolò Machiavelli, *The Prince,* trans. Harvey C. Mansfield, Jr.
(Chicago: University of Chicago Press, 1985), 101.

[7] Jacob Klein, *Greek Mathematical Thought and the Origin of Algebra,*
trans. Eva Brann (New York: Dover Publications. 1992). Subsequent references are given in parentheses in the text.

"Now what is characteristic of this 'general magnitude,'" writes Klein, "is its indeterminateness, of which...a concept can be formed only within the realm of symbolic procedure" (123). In other words, in the real world one never encounters a general magnitude, only specific *numbers of things*, even if there are too many to count easily. Klein discusses at length the "simple pregnancy" in Greek thought of the difference between one and two. The word *arithmos*, root of *arithmetic*, usually translated as "number," does not apply to one thing, for example. One is not a number at all. "In the process of counting...it is only *the multiplicity of the counted things* which is the object of attention. Only that can be 'counted' which is *not one*, which is before us in a certain number: neither an object of sense nor one 'pure' unit is a *number* of things or units. The unit as such is no *arithmos*....The smallest number of things or units is: *two* things or units. The unit itself is, of course, still smaller than the smallest number." Klein continues, "It is just because this is the case that it has the character of a 'beginning' or 'source' (*archē*) such as makes something of the nature of 'counting' originally possible" (49). The implication is that "one," without being a number itself, generates numbers, not "number" in the sense of general magnitude, but specific numbers. Klein argues that this is a critical distinction separating ancient mathematical thought from modern mathematics. By contrast, Euclidean geometry never replaces "the real determinateness of an object with a *possibility* of making it determinate." It is always engaged in "*illustrating* a determinate object" (123).

The distinction is crucial. When a geometer thinks of the pure properties of a rectangle, he can constantly refer to the drawn rectangle that illustrates it. In algebra, by contrast, the sign—x, for example—expresses *possible* determinacy within its system of formulas. A very intelligent bachelor I once knew had a complete list of the qualities any future wife of his must have. In other words, he had worked out a *possible* determinacy, and he actually spoke about such things as the "concatenation of causes" he anticipated in finding this posited Lady X. Not so with Odysseus and Penelope, one suspects, and not so with Dante, who might transhumanize Beatrice almost out of feminine existence in the *Paradiso*, but her meanings always refer back to the real person he met as a child in Florence, and he never entirely ceases to feel the ardor expressed in his early poems.

For the Greeks, even in the higher reaches of mathematics, numbers are always "counting-numbers," and there is no concept of "number" per se, no idea of "general magnitude." By contrast, as Klein writes of modern mathematics, the "concepts [of algebra] no longer have that natural range of meaning available in ordinary discourse, by an appeal to which a truer sense can always be distinguished from a series of less precise meanings." Rather, "nothing but the *internal connection* of all the concepts, their mutual relatedness...makes accessible to the understanding their... relevant...content" (120–21, emphasis added). In other words, the system and language of modern mathematics are self-contained, almost completely inaccessible to the layman. Greek geometry, by contrast, deals with shapes and numbers always discernible in the natural world, with constant reference to circles, triangles, squares, rectangles, cones, cylinders, spheres.

Raskolnikov's theory is algebraic by analogy, I am arguing. At first glance, it appears to arise from thinking about real men in history, but in fact, it begins with a single abstraction born of pride, the superiority of each great man, then opposes that abstraction to the supposed worthlessness of everyone else, and deduces a right to transgress the rules that bind the many. A specific person like Napoleon becomes a name in a theory, and the name then becomes the sign in a system whose internal connections make it compelling as long as it allows no distracting details from the real world into it. Raskolnikov's theory descends into the real world only because he needs to find the one relevant empirical validation of it: his own status as a subject, either extraordinary or common.

Six weeks before the murder, pressed by his poverty, Raskolnikov took his father's watch and a gold ring to Alëna Ivanovna, the first time he met her, and pawned them for two rubles. Immediately afterward, he overheard a student in a tavern talking to an acquaintance about the very woman he had just visited. "Kill her, take her money," the student said, "on condition that you dedicate yourself with its help to the service of humanity and the common good: don't you think that thousands of good deeds will wipe out one little, insignificant transgression? For one life taken, thousands saved from corruption and decay! One death, and a hundred lives in exchange— why, it's simple arithmetic!" (56). What struck Raskolnikov at the time was the coincidence of it, as though this other student had mirrored the idea in his own mind. *Something* outside his own will had done so, at any rate. Later, he tells Sonya, "I know myself that it was the devil dragging me along," but at the time, he saw only that the world had answered him in an uncanny way. Fortune provides him with the experiment he needs: killing an old woman. He comments to himself on the ugliness of it, even though he despises her: "Oh God, how repulsive! Can I possibly, can I possibly...no, that's nonsense, it's ridiculous!...How could such a horrible idea enter my mind?" (6). But in his system ugliness cannot be evidence of anything.

Alëna Ivanovna is mean-spirited, greedy, and suspicious. She keeps great sums of money, which represent power to act, out of the hands of those like him who might use it to great advantage. His own value will rise tenfold, a hundredfold, if he can liberate this power and become a benefactor. If it means killing her, so be it. In terms of the Gospels that his mother still reads, as do Sonya, Lizaveta, and Porfiry, among others, Raskolnikov and the pawnbroker are equal in sharing the image and likeness of God. In his system, such a teaching of equality merely holds back the great man. Hence the need for a "New Word." The beauty of an action no longer counts for anything.

But if it were merely a matter of becoming a benefactor, then he could simply steal the money. The whole point is killing her. He has the *obligation* to kill her if he wants to demonstrate and thereby liberate his greatness. Killing her, in itself, will be the proof of what was previously indeterminate. "Strength, strength is what I need," as he puts it at one point. "Nothing can be done without strength; and strength must be gained by strength" (161). In his picture of the world, everything depends upon the will to power, as we would say after Nietzsche. Raskolnikov recognizes that his calculations about Alëna Ivanovna Ivanovna will not be true unless he actually carries out the murder and breaks the law that holds his conscience in the old order. The proof of the math lies in what he proves *himself* to be, and the very character of what reality will be depends on the character of his subjectivity. His theory needs that point of intersection with the world of history. By actually murdering the old pawnbroker and taking her money, which the student he overheard would never dream of doing, he will demonstrate objectively his difference from ordinary men. Only by experiment will his difference be "empirically falsifiable," as Benedict says truth must be under the "self-imposed limitation of reason" (#56) that characterizes modern science.

The problem is that the theory will be falsifiable not as such but only with regard to him as the individual subject and source. Even if Raskolnikov cannot carry out the murder without committing the mistakes of ordinary criminals, which is obviously the case, the theory stands intact because Napoleon and Mahomet transgressed against the old order without hesitation or guilt. The deed tests whether he is extraordinary in the same way. Like Nietzsche two decades later, he projects before his imagination the *übermensch*. His obedience lies in obeying the law his reason sets out for him. Even if he falls short, he knows the truth only by experiment. As he confesses to Sonya, "I did not commit murder in order to use the profit and power to make myself a benefactor to humanity. Rubbish! ... What I needed to find out then, and find out as soon as possible, was whether I was a louse like everybody else or a man, whether I was capable of stepping over the barriers or not. Dared I stoop and take power or not? Was

I a trembling creature or had I the *right*..." (354). Even after the murders, this theoretical frame makes it impossible for him to see the nature of the deed he has already committed. As T. S. Eliot puts it in another context, he "had the experience but missed the meaning."

Raskolnikov's theory helps illuminate the justifications of the most murderous ideological tyrants of the twentieth century. What happens when his idea grips him illuminates the motives of terrorists in the twenty-first. The question is whether someone can step over the barriers and commit a violent deed to achieve an extraordinary standing. Such a person obeys the dictates of an idea but no longer answers to reason. Reflection suggests a powerful similarity between Raskolnikov's "New Word," distinctly Western and modern in tenor, and the abstraction with regard to human life that characterizes contemporary terrorism, which believes that it is attacking all the tenets of the modern West. Perhaps following a voluntarist god whose will "is not bound up with any of our categories, even that of rationality" (#14), and following the dictates of one's own will as a self-sufficient subject amount to the same thing.

At the heart of this similarity lies the question of the innocent, the *being* of others as opposed to their value in one's system. What Raskolnikov appears to forget throughout the novel, whenever he justifies himself theoretically, is that he also killed Alëna Ivanovna's sister, the innocent Lizaveta. His confession to Sonya earlier in the book specifically addresses who killed Lizaveta, not the old pawnbroker, but whenever he speaks from his theory, he always omits Lizaveta from the picture. Theoretically, it is one person he killed, not two. But the true object of his thought is never the old pawnbroker herself but an abstraction like the pure superiority of the great man, accessible only to thinking: an utterly vile, worthless human being. Her human qualities, for instance, the fact that she has "thin fair hair, just turning grey," or the evidence of her possessions, such as "an enormous case of icons" in her room, are irrelevant to him. Just before his confession in the police station, he cries to his sister, "Crime? What crime?...Killing a foul, noxious louse, that old moneylender, no good to anybody, who sucked the life-blood of the poor, so vile that killing her ought to bring absolution for forty sins—was that a crime?" (438). As for Lizaveta, she has never entered his theorizing at all, just his calculations, in the sense that he counts on her absence. She is good, a little simple-minded, and pregnant, oddly, as he overhears from the same student who first gave him the idea of killing the pawnbroker. It's a detail to ponder. In killing her, he takes two lives rather than one. Or rather, one murder becomes three, and suddenly the resonance is Trinitarian.

If Raskolnikov had met the old pawnbroker before he formulated his system, he would have disliked her anyway, but he would not have derived from her the idea of the extraordinary man and the necessity of killing her to prove himself one of them. The theoretical system, nurtured in his spider hole of a room, that denatured womb where his thinking slowly took on the form of a grisly crime, comes first. She dies because the transgression abstractly necessary, this possible determinacy with its x, has to be decided so that he can leave the old reality behind. Yet it does not happen in the way he intends. One turns into two, which is really three, and reality overspills the frame of his intention. Is it just that reality is messier than mathematics, or is there a deeper proportionality to be discovered? Upon reflection, we can see that Raskolnikov's use of Alëna Ivanovna has a simple pattern, the imposition of an idea on stubborn particulars. Yet in this context, his action begins to emerge as a demonic imitation of God's descent into history. His "New Word" comes into the world through a particular woman at the acceptable time, but in the sense that fortune is a woman who must be beaten—beaten to death.

Any parallel to the Incarnation would perhaps never occur to us, however, unless holy Lizaveta had turned up, apparently by accident, just in the way that such unanticipated things happen to the best-laid plans. As soon as she enters the apartment and Raskolnikov kills her, the nature of his transgression has the potential to reveal itself to him. This possible revelation differs from possible determinacy, because significance lies in the being of this person, in Lizaveta's pregnancy, with its echo of the Virgin, which is symbolic because it is real. Simply noticing her begins to bring the meaning out of concealment. Not only are Raskolnikov's murders a deadly algebra imposed on living human beings, but they are also and most powerfully revealed as an attempt to split the Word from the conditions of the body, to disincarnate it, to intellectualize it, and to seal this new covenant with a sacrifice. "You shall be as gods" is a very old temptation.

If everything had turned out as he planned, the old woman's death might have remained barren of further meaning for him, and the truth would have remained dead in Raskolnikov in that room of his, like Lazarus in his tomb. He has the experience and at first misses the meaning, but "approach to the meaning restores the experience / In a different form" as Eliot writes,[8] and that gradual approach comprises the remainder of the novel and its epilogues. As his story fits into the context of the lives around him, one has the

---

[8] T. S. Eliot, "The Dry Salvages," in *T. S. Eliot: The Complete Poems and Plays, 1909–1950* (New York: Harcourt, Brace and World, 1971), 133.

sense of something distorted now coming into its true proportions within the whole of reason and all its analogies. Raskolnikov's single picture of the world, though it lies at the center of the book, has many complementary and competing views alongside it, which Mikhail Bakhtin has called the polyphonic structure of Dostoevsky's novels. Identity in this novel never remains static, despite the attempts of the ego to hold itself intact. It keeps doubling and tripling. Dostoevsky gives us a world constantly mirroring and refracting itself. Marmeladov's family situation becomes a counterpart of Raskolnikov's, and Sonya, a double of his sister Dunya. At the same time, Sonya's stepping over the moral law also makes her resemble Raskolnikov, at least in his interpretation of her action. Luzhin and the monstrous Svidrigailov, who molests children, are both, in their different ways, counterparts of Raskolnikov, either in their ideas or in their deeds. But so is Razumikhin, and so, in his way, is Porfiry Petrovich, who tracks Raskolnikov through the theory to the ugly deed. As Razumikhin would say, "the living soul" cannot be reduced to algebra.

The presence of Porfiry Petrovich, whom I described earlier as a Socratic trickster, adds considerably to this righting of perspectives. Porfiry's concern, not just with the crime, but with the opinions of this intelligent young man, make Raskolnikov appear as a version of Callicles in the *Gorgias* or Thrasymachus in the *Republic*, a recognition that places the central arguments of what we have been describing as modern thought squarely within the dialogues of Plato. When the pope speaks of "modern scientific reason with its intrinsically Platonic element," he means not the Socratic correction of false opinions, as his quotation from the *Phaedo* clearly shows, but a movement toward treating the real world as secondary to a mathematical structure discernible in it. Yet even in this regard, as we have seen, the Greeks have a thoughtfulness not grounded in the individual subject and an indispensable difference. Klein elucidates: "In Greek science, concepts are formed in continual dependence on 'natural,' pre-scientific experience, from which the scientific concept is 'abstracted.' The meaning of this 'abstraction,' through which the conceptual character of any concept is determined, is *the* pressing ontological problem of antiquity" (120). This problem fades away completely in modernity, he says.

Crime and Punishment is only one of Dostoevsky's meditations on modernity and its forgetfulness of being. In *The Possessed*, he explores different versions of ideology in the liberal Stepan Trofimovich Verhovensky, his much more radical student Stavrogin, Stepan's socialist son Pyotr Verhovensky, and other related ideologues such as Kirilov, who interestingly believes that committing suicide will make him a god, and Shigalov, a kind of proto-Stalin. Ivan Karamazov, just one of Dostoevsky's characters in *The Brothers Karamazov*, has entered the canon on his own as the author of "The Grand Inquisitor." Dostoevsky has counterparts in Russian literature, nor is Russia alone in taking up the peculiar reductions and distortions of modernity. According to Kundera, "if it is true that philosophy and science have forgotten about man's being, it emerges all the more plainly that with Cervantes a great European art took shape that is nothing other than the investigation of this forgotten being.... [A]ll the great existential themes Heidegger analyzes in *Being and Time*—considering them to have been neglected by all earlier European philosophy—had been unveiled, displayed, illuminated by four centuries of the novel."[9] Kundera enumerates the explorations of the dimensions of being in the European novel, such as time past in Proust or time present in Joyce. In America, Hawthorne's stories such as "The Artist of the Beautiful" or "Rappaccini's Daughter" are allegories of the conquest of nature. Melville gives the same themes a cosmic theological scale in the epic action of *Moby-Dick*. Faulkner presents distinctive versions of modernity in such figures as Thomas Sutpen, Joe Christmas, and Flem Snopes, as well as exploring a troubled resistance to the whole modern project in Isaac McCaslin of *Go Down, Moses*. Flannery O'Connor writes about Raskolnikov's Georgia cousins, from Hazel Motes preaching the "Church without Christ" from the hood of his rat-colored car to the nihilistic Bible salesman of "Good Country People."

Since the late sixteenth century, modern literature has stubbornly shown the effects of turning the world into an object of use. Shakespeare and Marlowe both deploy the "Machiavel," for example, who tramples on moral conventions. The other dimension is the ennobling, if highly subjective, illusion of Cervantes's Quixote. In both cases, something has begun to change in the confident imagery of ascent that once characterized the movement toward contemplation, from Plato's cave through the *Dream of Scipio* to the *Divine Comedy* and into the neo-Platonists of the early Renaissance. When Dante inhabits the increasingly beautiful mathematical cosmos of the *Paradiso*, he does so with greater and greater illuminations of love, but in Dostoevsky, as in the pope's lecture, the mathematical model inherited from Descartes impinges reductively on the world of human action. What used to be, at its upper reaches, an increasingly simple seeing or beholding disappears before modern technology, which needs to *do* something to the world to prove itself.

[9] Kundera, 4–5.

If the crucial shift appears to lie in the relation between mathematics and the real world of things, the crucial correctives lie in our constant, thoughtful return to the Greeks and to revelation, but also to the kind of thinking that poetry affords us. Obviously, literature can fall prey to its own limitations of reason and its failures of imagination. But at its best, literature gives us the lived world and habituates us in what it means to think within the analogy of being, which underlies any movement "to engage the whole breadth of reason." Modern scientific thought may have led to a self-limitation of rationality, but what better, more healing way is there than a novel like *Crime and Punishment* to demonstrate, through its very action in the soul of the reader, that the Raskolnikov room, the womb of murder, is also the tomb of Lazarus? Those who call him out of it, the Socratic figure, Porfiry Petrovich, and the figure of Sonya, the mediatrix of grace, combine the two great strains of Greek reason and Christian revelation called for at Regensburg.

Rationality in Augustine's Confessions

Michael McShane

In the Regensburg Address, the Holy Father emphasizes the essential importance for Catholic Christianity of rationality in general and Greek philosophy in particular. Further, he reasonably emphasizes a real continuity between Greek philosophy and Catholic Christianity. In the context of this discussion, Benedict mentions the name *Augustine*, so I thought it might be useful to discuss some features of Augustine's understanding of Greek philosophy, as it appears in his *Confessions.* Benedict seems to emphasize the continuity between Christian theology and Greek philosophy in Augustine. In this paper, however, I will initially focus on what Augustine sees as the radical *discontinuity* between the two. Although it might seem as if my view is inconsistent with Benedict's on this matter, I will finally show a way in which the two are at one or are nearly so.

To begin, Benedict's Regensburg speech famously does not say many things that people thought it said, of course. For instance, he carefully did not affirm in his own voice the idea that what is original to Islam is evil and inhumane, as is well known. But he similarly does not clearly affirm that God does not crave the blood of infidels; that God's rationality does not allow forced conversion; that Islam is a voluntarist religion; that Augustine and Thomas are intellectualists; that Scotus is a voluntarist. Nor does he affirm in his own voice that it is *false* to say that what is original to Islam is evil and inhumane, for that matter, not in the text itself or in the clarifications he issued subsequently.

While Benedict neither affirms nor denies the above points, nonetheless, he does affirm, in his own voice, that there is "profound harmony between what is Greek in the best sense of the word and the Biblical understanding

of faith in God" (#17). But this in itself remains somewhat unclear, since
the Holy Father does not spell out exactly what he means by "profound
harmony" or, perhaps more important, by the expression "Greek in the best
sense of the word." Answering what is meant by "Greek in the best sense
of the word" is necessary in order to determine Augustine's view on Greek
rationality and will illuminate what the pope means by "profound harmony."
So this, precisely, is my task: to discover what it is that is "Greek in the
best sense of the word" that is also in a "profound harmony with" Catholic
Christianity, according to Benedict.

In his discussion of Christianity and Greek philosophy, it is note-worthy
that Benedict does *not* discuss a text that would seem to be centrally important, namely the discussion from Paul about how Christianity is "Foolishness to the Greeks" (1 Cor 1:23). Now Paul here is also difficult to
interpret, but it seems as if he is marking a radical *discontinuity* between
Greek philosophy and Christianity. Benedict, on the contrary, emphasizes
a continuity between Christianity and Greek philosophy.

Does the statement from Paul prove that Benedict is incorrect or that
his view is inconsistent with Paul's view? No. For again Benedict carefully says that he is interested in the harmony between the faith and what is
Greek "in the best sense of the word." So perhaps Benedict would be quick
to tell us that the Greeks to whom Christianity is foolishness do not represent what is Greek in that best sense. Still, it is puzzling that Benedict does
not explicitly mention this important statement from Paul on the Greeks.
In any case, it seems a way into a discussion of Augustine's views on rationality, particularly Greek rationality, and Christianity.

In the *Confessions*, Augustine's position on Greek philosophy initially
seems clear. In Book VII, Augustine implies that rationality alone
can get one as far as thinking of a certain kind of monotheism, for
instance:

> Through a man puffed up with monstrous pride, you brought under
> my eye some books of the Platonists, translated from Greek into
> Latin. There I read, not of course in these words, but with entirely
> the same sense and supported by numerous and varied reasons,
> "In the beginning was the Word and the Word was with God and
> the Word was God. He was in the beginning with God. All things
> were made by him, and without him nothing was made. What was
> made is life in him; and the life was the light of men. And the light
> shone in the darkness, and the darkness did not comprehend it."
> Moreover, the soul of man, although it bears witness of the light, is

"not that light," but God the Word is himself "the true light which illuminates every man coming into the world."*

However (as also shows up in this passage and the next one), Augustine appears to hold that there is a radical discontinuity between unaided rationality (both Greek and in general) and Christianity, since, he says, the Greeks did not reason their way to Christ as incarnated, crucified, and redeeming: "But that 'he took on himself the form of a servant and emptied himself, and was made in the likeness of men and found to behave as a man, and humbled himself being made obedient to death, even the death of the Cross so that God exalted him' from the dead . . . —that these books do not have" (VII.ix [14]). Indeed, Augustine indicates that there is something about those essential elements of Christianity that is not available to pure reason. Thus to the degree that one relied upon reason alone, as he sees it, the essential elements of Christian *doctrine* remain unavailable.

What is more, there seems to be nothing in unaided reason that will enable or encourage correctly humble and essentially Christian *attitudes* and actions such as glorifying God or giving him thanks. Arrogant philosophers who rely only on their own thoughts, then, are ultimately blocked from the most important truths and attitudes, and "professing themselves to be wise, they have become fools," says Augustine in VII.ix (14), quoting Romans 1: 21–3. So the passage discussed above seems to indicate that pure rationality is not sufficient to get one to distinctively Christian doctrines or attitudes, though it does seem to be sufficient to give a more or less accurate account of God the Father.

Elsewhere in the *Confessions*, Augustine points toward more and possibly deeper problems concerning the relationship between rationality and Christianity and even mere monotheism. In Book I, he asks: "Who then are you, my God?" He answers the question with rhetorical questions, saying: "What, I ask, but God who is Lord? For 'who is the Lord but the Lord?,' or 'who is God but our God?'" (I.iv [4]). This question-and-answer sequence can be multiply interpreted, but one plausible interpretation is this: The question "who is God" can somehow ultimately be answered only by means of tautologies: God is God.

From the point of view of logic, a tautology is generally one of two ways in which one cannot usefully make a statement. To the person who asks about God, not knowing the answer, a tautological reply is logically

* St. Augustine, *Confessions*, trans. Henry Chadwick (New York: Oxford, 1998), VII.ix (13). Subsequent references will be in parentheses in the text.

uninformative inasmuch as it simply *assumes* what is being asked. A tautology does not make a real statement from a strictly logical point of view; rather it simply stutters. Tautologies are always true, we learn from Wittgenstein, and thus they are useless for picturing what is empirically in the world. And this will later confirm something we already know, that God is not an empirical item in the empirical world.

(Here, if I had space, I would discuss the relationship between the tautology and the so-called Platonic Doctrine of Recollection from Plato's *Meno*. I believe that Augustine here signals to us that reasoning about God is tautologous in part because we all always already do know God but simply need to recollect Him. It is a question not of logical learning but of a kind of recognizing or remembering who we always already were and are and what our lives mean, something that we are set up in advance by God to be aware of but perhaps dimly. This is part of the significance of the possessive pronoun in the questioning answer "Who is God but *our* God?")

To return to the point, I mention that the tautology is one of two logically improper ways of making a statement. That there are two is significant because in the same passage examined above, Augustine then immediately goes on to engage the second logically improper way of making a statement, that is, logical contradiction. Tautologies, as we saw above, are logically useless because always true; contradictions, on the other hand, are always false, therefore nonsense, therefore also logically useless.

Thus, after saying God is God, Augustine offers a string of predicates concerning God. Some of them seem not inconsistent, such as "most high, utterly good." However, there are some sets of predicates that do seem to be deliberately inconsistent. For instance, he describes God in the following pairs: "always active, always in repose"; searching and lacking nothing; jealous and not anxious; repentant and without pain of regret; wrathful and tranquil. To take just one example, it would seem that jealousy is a kind of anxiety. Hence, in a straightforward reading, it is logically impossible to have jealousy without anxiety. It would be like saying one had chocolate cake but not any cake. The other examples mentioned above entail similar logical problems.

It is important to note that Augustine here does not parse these pairs in such a way that indicates he intends them as logical contradictions. It is possible that in each case we could very cleverly find some relevant respect, make a careful distinction, such that there is no contradiction. Still, the passage seems carefully constructed to appear as if it involves logical contradictions. Indeed, Augustine makes no attempt to disambiguate that appearance. He offers no sense in which God could logically be both jealous and not anxious, for instance, or wrathful but in some other respect or at some other time tranquil. I thus conclude that Augustine (concerned with theo-logic in this passage) intended precisely to move from a string of tautologies to a string of logical contradictions. And in the second part of that movement, by the way, Augustine mirrors an argument made by Socrates in Book II of the *Republic* (380e–383c), though I make no claim here that Augustine actually read that work.

I propose then that Augustine in this passage is working on the issue of the logical status of theo-logic. Other evidence in the passage confirms this proposal. One such piece of evidence is that among the list of predicates Augustine proposes here, one that appears prominently is that God is "incomprehensible." If ultimately theology must involve tautologies and contradictions, as I am interpreting this passage, then this would surely be consistent with the notion that God is, logically speaking, "incomprehensible," as Augustine states here.

The passage under consideration thus precisely concerns the possibility (or impossibility) of using language, *logos*, to speak of God. But there is further evidence for this thesis: after offering (what I take to be) his string of tautologies and contradictions, Augustine is quick to address a potential objection. He says, "But in these words what have I said, my God, my life, my holy sweetness? What has anyone achieved in words when he speaks about you?" Here with these rhetorical questions, Augustine imagines someone, a philosopher, making the following objection: "If theology is composed of tautologies and contradictions, then how can it qualify as an 'ology' at all? What is the point of saying anything at all in *logos* about God, if all that can be said is shot through with illogical nonsense and uninformative stuttering?" To this imagined philosopher's objection, however, Augustine's reply is swift and severe. He says: "Yet woe to those who are silent about you because though loquacious with verbosity they have nothing to say."

The last reply to the imagined objection more or less curses those (philosophers) who, out of deference to logic, remain silent about God, who refuse to proclaim God. The reply seems to indicate the following: Augustine makes a kind of ethical response to a question that expresses itself logically. Those who are "loquacious with verbosity" are, as ever in the *Confessions*, secular philosophers, worldly wise and ethically empty. Augustine indicates that it would be morally wrong and dangerous to allow the logic of the situation to trump the ethics of the situation. If one wishes to be on the right side of the Divine (and we all do, most radically even if sometimes unwittingly), then one must be willing to move from logic to ethics. In Augustine's teaching, then, logic is trumped by ethics, under-stood in the broadest sense. What one should *be* trumps what logic allows one to *comprehend*.

Finally, then, Augustine's point in the passage discussed above is to mark, right from its very outset, that the *Confessions* is a book that is simultaneously necessary and impossible. (I personally find this beautiful.) The book is spiritually necessary, since we are called to speak about God as best we can, and it would be a terrible and idolatrous error if we were silent about God only because logic ordered us to be so. But, Augustine seems to concede, from a purely logical point of view, theology per se is on shaky grounds. I take it, however, that this apparent concession means to him only that logic is not ultimate here. Logic, as Wittgenstein seems to have learned from Augustine, can determine how meaningfully to speak things that are empirically *in* the world, but logic cannot make any determination about "things" *beyond* the world. Augustine feels no Wittgensteinian com-punction to be silent about things that cannot be logically spoken. Instead, the entire *Confessions* is thus to be understood as Augustine being radically un-silent about that which cannot be logically spoken. The important thing is to speak in the proper mode, and that mode is prayerfully and humbly, aware that one is called to speak in a way that is beyond one's logical depths, so to speak.

To summarize: If reason equals logic, then it would look as if Augustine holds that rationality in general, and therefore Greek rationality in particu-lar, can have no decisive part either in what is essentially Christian (namely the Incarnation, the Eucharist, and so on) or even in what is essentially monotheistic (because of the contradictions). In that case, Augustine would be radically at odds with Benedict, who holds that the two are profoundly harmonious. If, however, there is a sense of reason that is not limited to mere logic, Augustine and Benedict could agree. Such a sense of reason is often to be met with in Greek philosophy, of course, and can be seen, for instance, in the *Symposium* and the *Republic*.

In Book VII, a few sections after he quotes Romans on foolish wise men, Augustine carefully traces for himself his own version of the lad-der of love from Plato's *Symposium*. I draw the reader's attention to the sentences where Augustine mentions that he is interested in the power by means of which the human mind (including logic) works: "This power, which in myself I found to be mutable, raised itself to the level of its own intelligence, and led my thinking out of the ruts of habit. It withdrew itself from the contradictory swarms of imaginative fantasies, so as to discover the light by which it was flooded" (VII.xvii [23]). If we can think at all,

Augustine reasons, this is because our rationality itself must stem from some higher source.

Four sections later, in Book VII, Augustine is again probing the source of human rationality. As he "began reading," he says, he "found that all the truth [he] had read in the Platonists was stated here together with the commendation of your grace, so that he who sees should 'not boast as if he had not received' both what he sees and also the power to see" (VII.xxi [27]). Philosophers should not be proud, he thus reasons, because they themselves did not invent rationality, did not invent logic itself, are not to be credited with the rationality of the world. Here Augustine again seemingly follows Socrates from the *Republic* in making a kind of transcendental argument: there must be something that is the source of intelligibility per se. That 'something' ultimately links the human mind with the world and makes the two of them harmonize to the degree that they do so. For Socrates, that source of rationality is called the Good; for Augustine, God. The differences are important, of course, but here I am marking the similarities. In either case, since the source of logic is itself not just another logical object in what we could call a logical field, it would make sense to say (if here it makes sense to say 'makes sense to say') that the source of logic itself is not itself subject to logic. Hence there is a kind of comfort in the idea that what is ultimate is in some sense rational—let's call it super-rational—but not necessarily logical. It transcends logic, we could say, as *nous* transcends *dianoia* in some Greek philosophy.

And here, as I see it, Benedict and Augustine finally do harmonize. In the Regensburg speech, when Benedict finally offers his critique of the most powerful modern rationality, he says that it is a kind of mixture of Platonic (by which I understand Pythagorean) rationality and empirical rationality. Benedict indicates the rationality, precisely, of the scientific method, by which one understands truth to be that which is mathematically countable (the Pythagorean part) and experimentally confirmable (the empirical part). His larger point, however, is that this form of rationality necessarily points beyond itself, since it makes ontological assumptions about the existence of the mathematical and the empirical orders as orders and about their correlation with the human mind. Such assumptions, Benedict says, must be interrogated rationally but cannot be interrogated in terms of the mathematical-empirical order itself. There is thus a kind of rationality that must transcend the rationality of empirical calculation. The rationality that he has in mind, I think, is the metaphysical rationality that pursues the Good or God. And surely this super-rationality is Greek (in precisely the best sense of the word) and surely it is Christian. From this point of view, then, it seems perhaps there is indeed a deep harmony among Socrates, Augustine, and Benedict.

One final point: the super-rationality spoken of above can also be called 'mystical.' As such, super-rationality will not, as I see it, be able to determine in any logically compelling way the answers to questions such as whether God craves the blood of infidels. Super-rationality cannot successfully engage such problems, for good or ill. It is just not that kind of thing. That same super-rationality, though, can lead to the sort of experiences spoken of in the final passage I wish to cite.

In Book X, Augustine says: "You called and cried out loud and shattered my deafness. You were radiant and resplendent, you put to flight my blindness. You were fragrant, and I drew in my breath and now pant after you. I tasted you, and I feel but hunger and thirst for you. You touched me, and I am set on fire to attain the peace which is yours" (X.xxvii [38]). This passage represents the merging of the most lyrical Christian love poetry with the most super-rational philosophical *noesis*. Such Augustinian writing seems to reflect a harmony of what is Christian and what is Greek, in the best sense of the word.

The Virtue of Docility

R. R. Reno

Is not this the error, the common and fatal error, of the world, to think itself the judge of Religious Truth without preparation of the heart?

—*John Henry Newman*

Nearly a decade ago, John Paul II circulated his reflections on the relation of faith and reason. The general tone of the encyclical, *Fides et Ratio,* was striking. Instead of throwing the weight of his office behind the legitimacy of faith against the encroaching criticisms of secular reason, John Paul devoted most of his arguments and exhortations toward the defense and encouragement of the life of reason. Pope Benedict's recent address to the faculty at the University of Regensburg struck a similar note. The former theology professor did not dig trenches around the domain of faith. Instead, he called for a renewed confidence in the power and scope of reason.

To a certain kind of reader, these papal defenses of reason must have seemed baffling. Hasn't news of secularization come to Rome? Are the writings of Richard Dawkins unknown to Vatican officials? Don't modern popes know that the sea of faith is receding, exposing what Matthew Arnold memorably described as the naked shingles of the world?

Christians always need to give reasons for the hope that is in them (1 Pt 3:15), but both John Paul's and Benedict's defenses of reason respond to the ironic turn of secular culture. During the Enlightenment and through most of the modern era, the disputed question concerned the source of authority: What will guide our lives? Should it be the old vision of reason directed and corrected by the authority of revelation, or should we live by reason alone? Thus, Voltaire wished to strangle the priests in order to free us to follow the pure dictates of reason. John Stuart Mill wanted to inculcate a spirit of critical intelligence so that we could overcome conventional moral categories and better serve the real needs of humanity. But times have changed. Today, the severe rationalism of the Enlightenment troubles the postmodern conscience nearly as deeply as the authority of the church. Both project a confidence in truth that our age increasingly regrets—and rejects.

John Paul II describes this new retreat from truth in pointed terms. He notes a "widespread skepticism" and "an undifferentiated pluralism." Both trends encourage us to become solipsists who imagine that "everything is reduced to opinion." He observes that our intellectual culture inculcates "attitudes of distrust of the human being's great capacity for knowledge." This distrust, John Paul worries, leads to "nihilism": we will not venture to live according to an existentially potent truth, because our age finds such truths dangerous, untrustworthy, and illusory.

The current pope seems largely to share John Paul's assessment. Before his election, Benedict memorably denounced what he called "a dictatorship of relativism," the paradoxical postmodern conviction that the one thing that must be true is the impossibility of truth. Or perhaps it is more accurate to say that the dictatorship of relativism asserts something more radical: the undesirability of truth. Not surprising, then, this relativism is more preached as a slogan than proposed for philosophical assessment. We must quiet the commanding voice of truth so that the permissive voices of difference can be heard. Or so we are told. Benedict analyzes the consequences differently. In a culture that "does not recognize anything as for certain," he observes that we slide toward egoism. Without the commanding truths that once disciplined and ennobled the soul, the raw imperatives of desire rotate to the center and set the agenda. We see the results today. A dictatorship of relativism takes the social form of hedonism, disciplined only by external systems of economic reward and punishment or, in hard cases, the police power of the state. Benedict returns to dangers of a relativistic culture in his Regensburg Address. There he reminds us of the threat of violent cultural conflict untempered by a common search for truth.

Undifferentiated pluralism, skepticism, relativism, nihilism, egoism, and the bloodthirsty sword: one cannot complain that the current teachings of the Catholic Church soft-pedal the depth and significance of the current crisis of reason. But is this syllabus of postmodern errors adequate? Benedict's formulation, "a dictatorship of relativism," certainly evokes a leveling sentiment that exerts a pervasive influence. My students, for example, are extremely anxious not to give the impression of imposing moral judgments on others, and discussions of current issues are hobbled by a tendency to dismiss arguments as mere expressions of opinion. But this functional relativism could hardly be described as a coherent or even conscious philosophical position, and criticizing it can feel like chasing a shadow. With this in mind, I want to press against an analysis of contemporary intellectual life that places too much emphasis on the role of bad theories of reason and truth. I will do so in order to clear some ground for what I hope will be a more plausible and helpful diagnosis.

Let's begin with *relativism* and *nihilism*. If we want to describe the contemporary university, then I'm afraid these terms do not help very much. The majority of professors are scientists of various sorts. They have a robust belief in the results of their disciplines, so much so that in my experience scientists seem largely uninhibited about telling others what is true. Part of the frustration one feels in reading Richard Dawkins comes from his cocksure confidence that the deliverances of science and his own sixty-second philosophizing can definitively settle age-old questions about God, the world, and the purposes of human life. But our exasperation should not blind us to the fact that natural scientists are consistently serious about truth. No dictatorship of relativism reigns in our university laboratories.

When we turn to the humanities, the situation changes. One can always find English professors who say that all truth claims are simply projections of power or who convey to their students the new academic mysticism of alterity and difference. But in nearly all cases, this apparent relativism is linked to an agenda-driven progressivism. Instead of contributing to an atmosphere of tentative uncertainty or paralyzing doubt, those who are most ardent in questioning truth are also those most likely to ally themselves with the intensely ideological goals of political correctness. The few who describe themselves as nihilists—Gianni Vattimo comes to mind—seem to have a similar, strangely contradictory profile. The actual tone of postmodern nihilism is moralistic rather than despairing, strident rather than tentative. Instead of concluding that life is meaninglessness, they urge their views as a transformative philosophy that will save our culture from its supposed addiction to tyranny and violence.

If we look beyond literary disciplines, we see that, in the English-speaking world, the discipline of philosophy is quite removed from the relativistic gestures or nihilistic postures of postmodernism. One need attend but a few faculty meetings to discover that philosophers are punctilious about arguments, and they can work themselves into fits of righteous indignation when they feel that reason is being betrayed. Even those who make the news with controversial positions fail to exhibit qualities one associates with relativism or nihilism. Peter Singer can be called many things but never a relativist. On the contrary, his utilitarianism yields a form of moral fundamentalism. John Rawls provides another example. His theory of justice may be based on impoverished assumptions about the human condition and the purposes of political life, but his basic intellectual concern is similar to the worry that motivated Benedict's Regensburg Address. Rawls sought to find a way for a commitment to reason to supervene in the potentially violent conflicts over the good that haunt our common life. Even Richard Rorty, whose rhetoric gives the impression of denying truth, testifies to a deep moral purpose. He argued that we must give up certain fantasies about truth so that we can focus on the kinds of reasons that actually help us live well. It's an argument that goes back at least to Montaigne and was winsomely put forward by Hume.

My goal is not to defend smug scientists, rabid utilitarians, liberal political theorists, or the deflationary humanism of Rorty. My point is much simpler. If we leave aside folks such as Stanley Fish, who are more notorious than influential, then we find that the charges of relativism and nihilism miss the mark. Our intellectual culture may be inadequate and wrong-headed. I think it is. But that culture does not seem to be either relativistic or nihilistic in any ordinary sense of those terms.

How, then, should we proceed? Is the crisis of reason an illusion? Is all well in the contemporary university? Should we conclude that John Paul and Benedict mislead us? I think not. Let's go back and take another look at their diagnosis, for it suggests a fuller vision, both of the problems we face and the remedies we need.

It is important to recognize that both John Paul and Benedict embed terms such as *skepticism*, *relativism*, and *nihilism* in broader frameworks. In *Fides et Ratio*, John Paul consistently returns to an account of the current situation that reflects his deepest concern: we lack intellectual ambition. Our universities inculcate many forms of academic rigor. The modern scientific project churns forward. But by his reckoning, we increasingly neglect questions about what he calls "the ultimate and overarching meaning of life."

We see a similar concern in Benedict's Regensburg Address. The Pope opens with a fond recollection of the community of scholarship that influenced his development as a young professor. To be sure, he had religiously skeptical colleagues. It was not as though the Regensburg faculty in 1960 was of one mind. Yet they were united in the conviction that they could (and should) discuss a wide range of questions, including theological questions about the ultimate purposes of human life. In other words, across their real differences Benedict remembers a "profound sense of coherence within the universe of reason." He worries that today this intellectual concord has been lost. It is not the case that the scientists despair of truth or even that the philosophers and theologians have embraced relativism, though in the spirit of Matthew 7:5—"Thou hypocrite, first cast out the beam out of thine own eye"—Benedict has some pointed things to say about modern theology. Rather than relativism, he suggests that we have lost the confidence that the disciplines of the modern university—disciplines that have achieved remarkable sophistication and produce men and women of great intellectual refinement—can come together to help us understand how we should live our lives. The total moral and spiritual achievement of our contemporary intellectual training is far less than the sum of its parts.

Thus it seems to me that recent papal expressions of concern about the crisis of reason in the West tend to treat it as a matter of ambition and scope. We do not so much reject truth as retreat from what Benedict calls its "grandeur." The natural scientists continue with confidence. A similar spirit of energetic inquiry holds true for most social scientists, historians, and, as I have argued, nearly all philosophers. They manifest a commitment to objectivity and accuracy that should be cherished. Yet while most faculty are quite confident that reason can guide us toward a genuine command of the subject matter within individual disciplines, we suspect that reason cannot guide us toward mastery of our souls, and we worry that reason cannot govern our common life in a pluralistic world. This suspicion and worry infiltrates our academic culture. We are eager to convey to students knowledge of the laws of nature, social systems, and historical facts, but we separate education from the training of conscience. Expertise with facts, our intellectual habits of mind assume, is quite separate from competence in values. In this way, reason has not been denied; it has been de-moralized. Our universities are less hotbeds of relativism and nihilism than places where moral and spiritual questions go unasked and unanswered.

At this point I want to emphasize that tracking down and refuting bad theories is a worthwhile undertaking. Skepticism and relativism contribute to our sense that reason lacks moral competence. It is hard to give oneself over to the difficult work of seeking that which one thinks either unattainable or illusory. The same holds for unrealistic standards of proof and evidence. Restricting reason to formal proofs and experimental verification can be as much of a threat as relativism to an educational culture committed to the full development of reason, indeed, perhaps more of a threat, since our always imperfectly developed capacity for moral judgment is easily overawed by the achievements of science. Restoring the grandeur of reason will no doubt require criticisms of these views.

Nonetheless, while I concede, I must also caution. Refuting bad philosophical theories and replacing them with good ones turns out to be much less consequential than one at first imagines. John Henry Newman had a fine mind, and his critics often expressed frustration with the complex webs of distinction and inference that characterize his work. Yet Newman knew the limits of arguments. Reason, he observed, is critical but not creative. It can judge but not originate. It offers analysis to the mind but not motives to the soul (see Sermon 10, para. 13). As important as reason-giving is for our search for the truth, it interacts with a larger force that Newman often calls the power of "personality." Formal arguments and proofs do little to shape the mind. The intellect is cultivated, not surprisingly, by culture. Mutual sympathies, passionate loyalties, the excitement of the lecture hall, the intimacy of the seminar room, endless conversations in dorm rooms: these and countless other aspects of a vibrant intellectual community give life to reason. Our minds take on interests and form opinions by exposure to men and women who are themselves cultured, that is to say, teachers who are living representatives of a past that reaches forward through them to claim the young.

My colleagues in the natural sciences recognize the importance of personality, though they aren't likely to use Newman's term. They complain about compliant students who memorize scientific doctrines but fail to manifest the spirit of scientific inquiry. They know that the students have the wrong attitudes, not the wrong ideas. Students suffer from the wrong habits of mind and not the wrong theories. In a certain sense, then, they must be converted rather than convinced. They need to be influenced and formed, not informed and instructed. This holds for all students and not just those who want to go to medical school and who treat science classes as, at best, sources of useful technical knowledge to be mastered or, at worst, as hoops to jump through. A good education does not satisfy interests; it shapes them. It does not help students achieve their goals. A good education tries to guide and shape their goals. A healthy academic community is a school as much of desire as of the mind, or, more accurately, it is a school of desire because of the mind. For at its best, the mind is governed by a desire for truth, and this desire must be nurtured and directed, while other, corrupting desires need to be pruned and uprooted.

In the early Christian tradition, the virtue that guides our desire for knowledge was called *studiositas,* or studiousness. Traditional accounts of studiousness and its associated vices, curiosity and laziness, provide rich resources for assessing contemporary academic life. But I want to consider the virtue of *docilitas,* or docility, instead. Docility literally means the capacity to be guided or led. It is the virtue most relevant to moral formation. It disposes us toward the influence of what Newman calls personality. This connection suggests that reflecting on our present lack of docility will bring us more directly to an assessment of the crisis of reason we currently face.

St. Thomas Aquinas treats docility in his larger discussion of prudence, the virtue that guides us down the paths of wise action. Acquiring a good understanding of how to live well is not easy, however. At this point Thomas quotes Aristotle to the effect that we rightly pay close attention to the opinions of those more experienced and wiser than ourselves because they have accumulated a lifetime of wisdom about how to order their lives. The virtue of docility is thus a rightful attention and openness to instruction by those wiser than oneself. The docile mind is not overly credulous and slavishly devoted to particular individuals or schools of thought, but at the same time the docile mind is not closed to good influences. Sensitive to the ways in which the fallible human intellect needs assistance in order to make progress in figuring out how to live well, the docile student seeks good teachers in the hope of finding guidance (*Summa Theologiae* II–II.49.3).

The special role that St. Thomas assigned to docility in the development of practical wisdom is suggestive, pointing us toward the troubling feature of our present age. We don't lack for docility in the sciences. Students and teachers seem to possess a positive attitude toward the collective authority of the scientific community. And rightly so, for the authority of science arises from our judgment that the scientific authorities are not making things up. Not only are they well taught themselves, but we sense that scientists are, if I can be permitted an extension of the term, docile to the data they study. The natural scientists, we assume (rightly, I think), allow themselves to receive instruction from reality. Yet in the consideration of the proper ends of human action, we find a much different state of affairs today. When it comes to moral questions, broadly understood, neither students nor teachers sit at the feet of the older folks whose voices are kept alive in the great books of the past. In a word, we seem indocile to tradition.

A rejection of the authority of the past has long been a crucial feature of modernity, perhaps *the* crucial feature. As I observed at the outset, much changes in the shift from modern preoccupations with the perceived conflict between reason and the older authorities of Christendom to our present, postmodern anxieties about any form of command. But there is a line that connects the rationalism of Descartes to the apparently antithetical deconstruction of Derrida. For both, and for those who come in between, the past is received as a troublesome and unreliable inheritance that must be managed by new strategies of reason. The inevitable consequence of the

managerial approach is an insulation of the educated mind from the influence of personality, which is to say, the influence of inherited culture.

Let's look more closely at this underlying dynamic. In the older, Enlightenment phase, the promise was that reason would take the place of inherited authorities. We would guide our lives by method rather than judgment,
by deduction rather than discernment, by intelligence rather than virtue.
Utilitarianism is a clear instance. It proposes to replace conscience with
calculation. Postmodern deconstruction can seem very different, but it continues in the same relationship to culture. Instead of accepting the primary
role of inherited culture for moral formation, postmodernity has sustained
the basic form of the modern dream of reason. We are to theorize our way
to a humane life rather than submit ourselves to instruction from the past.
This attitude helps explain the political urgency, the smell of dictatorship,
that we find in the rhetoric of relativism. The promise is simple: If we no
longer believe in the good, then we will no longer have the impulse to fight
over the good. With the right theory of moral truth, that is to say, with the
theory of its nonexistence, we are delivered from our moral problems.

In this sense, although he firmly believes in moral truth, Peter Singer
is in the same boat as postmodern deniers of truth. Both utilitarianism and
the dictatorship of relativism endorse the promise of reason. If we have the
correct theory of truth or the good or the right, or for that matter the correct
theory of signs or culture or politics, then we will no longer need to enter
into the laborious (and always imperfect) task of forming our consciences
and disciplining our wills by way of the influence of older opinions about
how to live. No matter if one is a Marxist or a poststructuralist, a logical-
positivist or a latter-day skeptic, the basic educational dynamic remains
the same. Theory takes the place of personality as the source for guidance
about how to live. Not surprising, then, critical reflection, which is but a
word for the acquisition and application of theory, supplants the virtue of
docility as the habit we encourage in students—and in ourselves.

I don't want to give the impression that I am opposed to theories. They are
powerful tools for analysis, and they play an indispensable role in holding
together any sophisticated view of the world. Their role in the natural sciences is obvious. Data collection is important, for one can hardly explain
what one cannot see. But explaining matters more. It will not do merely
to chart the movements of the planets; the astrologers do as much. To be a
scientist one must also grasp the principle of gravity. But reflective scientists
are aware of the dangers of theories, whose central importance in modern
science can bewitch. One can be so ravished by the cognitive power and

elegance of a theory that one forgets that it serves the mind's desire to know the world. This is why science makes experimental fruitfulness such a decisive test for theory. The best theories guide experimental designs that deepen and expand our intimacy with the matter under investigation. Ideally, theory focuses the experimental isolation of phenomena, and in this way, theory intensifies the power of the natural world over the mind of the scientist. When functioning properly, scientific theories heighten the docility of the scientist to that which he wants above all to serve as the guide for his mind, which is, of course, the natural world itself.

The single most important development in higher education over recent decades has been the explosion of theory in the study of literature. Viewed superficially, the emergence of postmodern literary theories can be explained as an attempt by humanists to imitate the well-funded and powerful scientific disciplines. By this line of thinking, art history professors want to inject objectivity and discipline into their work, or at least appear to do so. I think a closer look shows otherwise. In the humanities theory plays a role very different from the one it has in the natural or social sciences, and this role renders contemporary academic life indocile to culture.

The dynamic is simple. In the sciences, theory returns the mind of the inquirer back to the material under study. In contemporary humanistic study, theory redirects intellectual interest toward cultural processes, either those at work within the coded structures of the work (e.g., deconstruction) or those that led to the artifacts' production and influence (e.g., old-fashioned historicism or new-fangled postcolonialism). In other words, scientific theory will take a young person's interest in the stars, and it will sharpen, deepen, and intensify that interest with powerful explanations of what aroused his intellectual desire in the first place. The star-gazing youth becomes an astronomer. In contrast, the role of theory in humanistic study is to induce in a young person a change of intellectual direction. "You used to think that the content of what you read mattered most," says the theorizing educator, "but in fact what you really need to know is how that content was produced, encoded, and made into a so-called truth that wants to gain control over your moral imagination." In short, theory in the humanities turns readers into analysts.

Consider a hypothetical undergraduate who reads Henry James's *The Bostonians*. With inchoate thoughts about the way in which James seems to commend the virtues of the parlor room over the triumphs of the parliamentary chamber, the student signs up for a class on James. He arrives and is delighted to discover that the class will focus on *The Bostonians*.

The works of some Marxist critical theorists are assigned, and he is asked to write a paper on the role of class identity in James. After readings in Levinas, another assignment directs his attention to the Southerner Basil Ransom as the agent of otherness. Derrida comes at the end of the syllabus, and our imaginary student, who is quite bright and quick to understand what the professor wants, develops a final paper that explains how the novel sets up a binary opposition between male (Ransom) and female (Olive Chancellor) that allows James to evade the ambivalent sexual identity of the object of the contest between them, Verena Tarrant. He gets an A for the class and encouragement to consider majoring in literature.

I want to be clear about the picture I have painted. I don't disdain the teaching of good theories any more than I reject the criticizing of bad ones. Each dimension of the imaginary class is legitimate on its own terms. For a close reading of James's novels, it pays to gain a more sophisticated understanding of the dynamics of class identity. Levinas is well worth attention, and Derrida's methods of reading are highly relevant to James. As James tells us in the introductions he wrote for the New York Edition of his novels, he thought in terms of character systems, an approach that sounds a lot like Derrida's theory of textual meaning. But notice how theory is deployed in relation to the novel in the course I have imagined. *The Bostonians* provides raw material to be operated upon and organized according to theoretical principles. The object of study is not the novel in itself but rather the cultural or semiotic processes that it represents.

Again, I want to be clear. There is nothing wrong with training students to be sociologically or semiotically astute. It is good to be reflective about all aspects of the human condition. Instead, I want to draw attention to the trajectory of my hypothetical student, a trajectory now widely encouraged in our educational culture. He starts out with an inchoate set of questions about what James had to say about the good and bad ways to live, but the course syllabus shifts his attention. What began as a moral interest, broadly understood, becomes something else. Training in cultural analysis takes the place of educating him about how to live.

The contrast to the role of theory in science is telling. Unlike the astronomer whose young love of the mystery of the stars is fulfilled by a lifetime as an astronomer, the young reader who was smitten by the power of Henry James's complicated, evasive, but powerful voice does not find his first love deepened and made more sophisticated by the reflection encouraged by a typical postmodern course in literature. This difference explains a fact evident to all. Theory in cultural studies does not help us become better readers.

Seeing this shift and the role of theory in the humanities has helped me understand the present crisis of reason, which is really a crisis of reason with respect to pressing cultural questions and not a crisis in molecular biology. According to Aristotle, the full dignity of our rational capacity is not found in our ability to solve mathematical equations. In fact, none of the qualities of mind encouraged by our present educational culture—critical reflection, theoretical sophistication, disciplined observation—describe the highest vocation of humanity. It is politics, says Aristotle, that provides the occasion for the fullest use of reason. By politics he does not mean polling data, fund raising, and spin. Instead, politics describes the human project of debating and deliberating about how to live. This project is what Benedict means by the grandeur of reason. It is the task of bringing all the real but subordinate intellectual achievements and mental habits of the contemporary intellectual life to bear on the political question, understood in the broad, Aristotelian sense, to which Benedict adds the theological question of what, ultimately, we should seek and serve. Culture is nothing other than the collective, enduring form of this theo-political project.

We are not born wise. We need to be trained to think intelligently about how to live, and as St. Thomas points out, this requires us to be docile to instruction from those who are older and wiser. We need to enter into the theo-political project rather than operating upon it critically from the outside. The full dignity of reason requires us actually to listen to what others say about how to live and to allow their claims to exercise an influence on our own convictions. The same holds for the past: we have to subject ourselves to culture and the influence of its personality. This is the essence of docility, and it is this disposition that we seem to lack. Our age does not want to train us to read Henry James as a person engaged in the age-old debate about how to live. Instead, we are encouraged to frame his work, and all other works, with a theory of culture. A desire for knowingness takes the place of the quest for wisdom. We may have cultivated that docility with respect to the natural world. The success of the modern scientific project strongly suggests that we have. But we are no longer docile to inherited culture. Therein, perhaps, lies our problem. We feel the impotence of reason with respect to moral and spiritual questions because we will not allow ourselves to be trained and instructed by the competent teachers of our tradition, or for that matter by teachers from any other tradition.

At the end of *Fides et Ratio*, John Paul II offers a meditation on the Virgin Mary. The vocation of the Virgin, John Paul writes, is in "deep harmony" with the proper vocation of philosophy. She offered her womb so that God's

Word might become flesh and redeem our humanity. In a similar manner, philosophy should open itself to God's revelation. And just as the Virgin "lost nothing of her true humanity and freedom," John Paul writes, "so too when philosophy heeds the summons of the Gospel's truth its autonomy is in no way impaired." He concludes, "Indeed, it is then that philosophy sees all its enquiries rise to their highest expression."[1] The vocation of Mary neither stymies nor short-circuits the full development of the human intellect. On the contrary, as John Paul's parable promises, her vocation realizes and perfects the life of reason. Thus, John Paul exhorts us to philosophize in Mary, and he ends the encyclical with a prayer to the Virgin as the Seat of Wisdom, petitioning her to intercede on our behalf and free us from all that hinders our search for the truth.

At first glance, the image is perplexing. One has difficulty imagining what philosophical insights the Virgin Mary might contribute to a scholarly discussion. St. Thomas or St. Bonaventure would seem more likely patrons of reason. One searches the Scriptures for any evidence of important truths that the Virgin Mary might give us as the basis for our intellectual lives. Why did John Paul not turn to St. John and the rich metaphysical content of the fourth Gospel? But it seems that the late pope was not interested in drawing attention to the specific teachings that theology might contribute to contemporary scholarly discussions. Instead of true doctrines or even reliable methods, in the Virgin Mary we see the perfect image of a virtuous disposition, one that is indispensable for the full development of reason. She gratefully receives that which she does not understand, what she cannot understand. She gives herself over to the service of God's Word, which is the source and ground of all truth, and she does so without reserve. She is, in a word, docile.

The intellectual life is different from Mary's position in important ways. We should never dispose ourselves toward teachers or books or artworks or any worldly authority with such self-abandoning trust. Our critical age rightly teaches us to interrogate and question the claims that our culture makes on our souls. Yet the critical moment is not sufficient. Today, we need to recover the virtue of docility in the intellectual life because without it we cannot be instructed about how to live. Here faith provides our age with the training it needs. Anyone who gives himself or herself over to prayer and worship enters into the Virgin's docility. To listen to the Scriptures as the Word of God, to receive the bread and wine as Christ's body and blood: these are dispositions of the soul that prepare us to receive and

---

[1] John Paul II, *Fides et Ratio* (Boston: Pauline, 1998), #108.

to be formed. These dispositions, central to the spiritual life, also leaven the intellectual life, and it is precisely the habit of docility that we need to nurture in order to re-open the soul of the contemporary university to instruction by the good teachers whose voices live in the culture we inherit. Perhaps, then, if I might echo John Paul, our goal should be to educate in the spirit of Mary, and our prayer should be for her kind intercession on behalf of our feeble, halting, and undoubtedly inadequate efforts to overcome the limitations of our indocile age.

The Courage of Reason and the Scandal of Education

Mary Mumbach

At the center of Pope Benedict's Regensburg Address is the daring admonition and assurance that the most immediate, even the greatest contribution to world peace that we in academia can make is to prepare for the classes meeting next Monday morning. We owe no apologies for total dedication to a task that, as his predecessor reminded us, issues from the very heart of the Church. If the pope's first encyclical, on love, seemed specifically, though hardly exclusively, addressed to spouses, his Regensburg Address gives a clarion call to us who work among those aspiring to be good bachelors, masters, and doctors of arts and sciences. What appeared most striking in 2006 when the address appeared in the news was the tremendous risk he took in delivering it, the testimony, the call to courage that Benedict was making to all of us in the academic life. Donald Cowan called the classroom a "sacred space," a "temple with doors closed so that learning can be celebrated." That James Schall begins his book on the address by emphasizing its specific identity as a university lecture rather than an encyclical, a homily, or a call to action, noting particularly its presentation on a campus, a space set apart from the streets, apart from the sway of power, connects it to this sacred space. It is delivered by a man not clinging to his status as pope but emphasizing his continued dedication to the role of professor, accepting the risks that it entails; its context is academic conversation among colleagues who may possibly have in common only the single but crucial acknowledgment of the life of reason. Was his affirmation a sin against charity? Schall says that in academic institutions, in that space set aside for the intellectual life, Benedict was reminding us that we are not just permitted but obliged to discuss such questions—questions that might be not only dangerous but even uncharitable to discuss in the streets. It is unlikely that he would have discussed ideas in the address while a guest at dinner in an Islamic home or used them as talking points in an interview with Larry King. Indeed, the importance of the solidarity that Professor Benedict expresses with those of us in this particular vocation should give us pause, for as Schall also notes, the virtue that he specifies as necessary for the intellectual life is courage. Celebration of the life of reason in an academic institution should diminish our risk but can never eliminate it.

"The courage to engage the whole breadth of reason, and not the denial of its grandeur—this is the programme with which a theology grounded in Biblical faith enters into the debates of our time....It is to this great *logos*, to this breadth of reason, that we invite our partners in the dialogue of cultures. To rediscover it constantly is the great task of the university" (#62–#63). This pope is the Cardinal Ratzinger who identified the chief subject of his predecessor=s encyclical entitled *Faith and Reason* to be "the adventure of truth." Courage is the virtue he cites as necessary for academics to proceed in their work, a virtue commonly associated, obviously, with the practice of the military profession, as Schall notes, and, one might add, with the witness, the professing of martyrdom. As certain commentators have recognized, the delivery of his speech, far from being a naïve unmindfulness (or even forgetfulness) of diplomacy, required a courage deliberately embraced. In fact, it seems to me a risk taken in our stead. There have been more than suggestions that speaking as he did might lead to his own martyrdom, and his speech did, in fact, lead to egregious acts of violent retribution, even to the murder of an innocent. It is a sign of our times that we must be reminded so violently of the day-to-day act of sacrifice, seldom referred to explicitly, which lies at the heart of the enterprise of education. Clearly, not the military but the academic life lived as he advocates gave him the habit of exercising courage both within and outside of the academy. Both the speech and the delivery of it indicate that growing in courage is at the heart of education rightly understood.

Benedict identifies the launch of his own adventure of truth and his training ground for courage as the peaceful classroom (and what I guess we=d call the faculty lounge, where colleagues gather). That the courage is ordinarily hidden gracefully in the peaceful campus settings, beneath the rituals, courtesies, and customs of the academic traditions, makes it, if anything, even more real. The veil of serenity covering the adventure has been lifted rather often lately to reveal the danger of our life in school: the imposition of political correctness and the alarmingly more frequent incidents of physical violence that have intruded into classroom settings recently. These are not random acts of violence, for surely they are symptomatic of a thirst for justice through power, in increasing despair of the efficacy of reason, as a result of the reduction of reason he elaborates on in his address. What impels Benedict to open his speech by recalling and treasuring the peace, the simplicity of the young institution in which he once exercised courage participating in the adventure of truth is not the desire to provide a homey or nostalgic touch, not an attempt to warm up the audience or to ingratiate himself with his hosts but an expression of gratitude and of joy. The facilities were austere; not even secretaries were provided. All the more impressive is his vivid memory of the essential, conversation with students and with other "ordinary" faculty, passionate and polite, even among those in the same discipline who disagreed with each other about ultimate matters, often, of course about faith, some disagreeing about everything except the reasonable basis of their adventure together.

The classroom, the faculty lounge, the lecture hall—all are part of the university, the free and open setting that for centuries has encouraged discourse, dialogue, questioning, exploration, and all the other modes of discovery that use reason. Such spaces are indeed sacred, for they allow teachers and students the opportunity to take risks, to take paths of exploration without repercussions, to test ideas, to forge their character in the process (as John Henry, Cardinal Newman argued), all in the attitude, the amplitude of love (*caritas*), without which reason cannot work well, if at all. There is magic when students comprehend the connections between Plato's cave, the divided line, and the sun metaphor and excitedly explain it to others and apply its understanding of how we know to their own activity. There is certainly magic in a Shakespeare class, for instance, in which students doing a close reading of *Othello* catch the echoes of Satan and Eve in the temptation of the Moor by Iago and then challenge each other point by point in working to understand why Shakespeare uses this reference. They come to know in the action of the play the devastation wrought by Iago's reduction of reason to a tool of manipulation that destroys the possibility of the dialogue of culture embodied in the marriage of Othello and Desdemona.

Such a glowing picture presents the wonders possible in the university when love and *logos*—and love of the *logos*—characterize and bind the community of the classroom and of the university. That we can enter into such a relationship is a gift that goes back to Socrates. We can trace the advent of institutions of higher learning and the campuses it is important that they be provided with to the sacrifice, both loving and reasonable, that

Socrates made. After he was executed for his teachings (and because he loved Athens and its laws, refusing to save his life by going into exile), the city itself was troubled that conversation in its streets had resulted in his death and, in effect, said: We will not insist that teachers daily risk execution for exploring truths that society might (rightly) consider dangerous to civil life if carelessly uttered or taken out of context on the street or in the marketplace. We will instead set aside a space for learning, for exploration, where otherwise dangerous or scandalous discussion may be enacted, minimizing the risk of violence based on misunderstanding. Thus, the Academy; thus, the Lyceum; and later, thus the medieval university, modeled on the monastery, the enclosed space, where truth could be celebrated, as Donald Cowan has asserted. Following the model of Socrates into our own time, academic freedom is bought, if you will, with our presumed willingness to sacrifice ourselves for the truth, though society (through the university) usually makes it possible not to have that ultimate sacrifice exacted. Benedict spoke in what was meant to be just such a safe place. Why then did violence and scandal occur?

In a nutshell, the Regensburg Address reminds us of the vulnerability of reason and the educational enterprise it engenders. All of us who participate in that enterprise expose ourselves to danger, scandal, and, yes, even death. What happens if a student misunderstands the classroom or the ideas discussed within it and violently disagrees with the process of education? Usually, the student will drop the class, but the potential for violence remains. The question we have to answer in this situation is "what ideas would we give our lives for?"

Violence did ensue, specifically death threats and the murder of a nun, over Benedict's defense of Greek reason. Implicit in his personal witness is that precise question that we all have to face now and then: would we risk dying for the heritage of Greece or for its manifestations in St. Augustine, Shakespeare, or our Founding Fathers? Do we remember that countless others have given their lives, not excepting the scribes who spent obscure lives copying manuscripts so that we might someday discuss the ever more easily accessible texts we assign so freely for each class we teach? I suspect that if Benedict had muted his message, had been defending, say, Thomas Aquinas or perhaps Dante, there would have been fewer who questioned his prudence. But to risk death and scandal in defense of the contribution of Socrates, Plato, Aristotle?—pagans! Yet Benedict knew well that St. Thomas and our long tradition of reason owed its existence to these pagan thinkers. It would be a sin of ingratitude if he did not acknowledge their places in our own lives, as Dante acknowledged, with exuberant gratitude, his debt to Virgil, his guide. In particular, it must have seemed that the least he could do in response to Socrates' sacrifice would be to risk his own life and reputation. In giving this lecture, Benedict himself has reminded us of the obligation of gratitude for the usually hidden spirit of sacrifice that underlies and makes possible our academic lives, which are, normally, unbloody sacrifices. He has reminded us of the ultimate value of our institutions, bought with a price others have been more than willing to give.

We are acutely aware of the attacks from the outside, the attacks of terrorists or even rationalists, but this lecture should resonate in our own minds with the sense of the danger from within as well. If we are tempted to take less seriously the life of reason because we have faith, Benedict shows us that to do so would be to deny the *logos* revealed in our very calling. We may be tempted to regard our various disciplines as secondary to other important matters in our lives in order to avoid the scandal of being mistaken for idolaters in our dedication to them. Most of us would like to think that we would die for love of country, faith, freedom, family, friends, though we fervently hope it never comes to that. Pope Benedict makes us question what ideas we would give up our lives for. He has given witness to a reality that is the basis for the privilege of our enjoying the academic life; he might even be said to have risked his life and reputation for the sake of Greek thinkers who first exalted and explored the territory of reason. Would we be willing to make the same sacrifice? Would we be willing to put our lives on the line for Socrates and, by implication, Homer? For *Utopia*? For Augustine's *Confessions,* Shakespeare's plays, Faulkner's novels? Would we encourage our students to do so? In risking his life and reputation, Benedict revealed part of the hidden foundation of our privilege of learning and teaching, the risk at the foundation of academic freedom.

There is another aspect to the sacrifice that a teacher makes. Most of us are not asked actually to die at the hands of colleagues, townspeople, deranged terrorists, or even students, though the great southern writer Caroline Gordon had a rather spectacular example of that kind of death. She relished giving the account of Cassian of Imola, a Latin grammar teacher in Rome. When discovered to be an early and secret convert to Christianity, he was sentenced to be stabbed to death by his students with their styluses. *Butler's Lives* indicates that the students had an ulterior motive for becoming his willing executioners: "They hated him, because he taught them well." In case anyone had any illusions about the objectivity of students' opinions in ratemyprofessors.com, the details of Cassian's sacrifice, particularly in that his teaching them well aroused their ire, proves otherwise. Nowadays our sacrifice commonly takes the form of accepting the (somewhat affectionate) ridicule of the world, which wants to know why, particularly if we teach in the liberal arts curriculum, if we are so smart, we aren't rich. We recognize the condescension that the world frequently (and, to tell the truth, at times with some justice) can take toward us; we know the look that says, "Poor thing, you just didn't know any better than to choose a life of escapism." Such little humiliations that bite and sting may prevent us from taking ourselves too seriously.

I mentioned earlier that teachers in the university are exposed to danger, especially to death, and scandal. I would like to conclude my discussion with a focus on the scandal—the truly creative, grace-filled kind of scandal—that teaching in a university should engender. To return to Benedict, perhaps the most shocking aspect of his Regensburg Address was the risk of scandal he accepted: Was this professor being unecumenical, if not actually uncharitable as many protested, risking offending others by quoting the words of a fourteenth-century emperor even though he gave the context and made it clear that he himself wouldn't have said what the emperor said? Most of us know what it's like to be quoted out of context, and being pope raised that risk for Professor Benedict. If it's done humorously, affectionately, it is part of a long tradition of satire in education, a sign not only of wit but of our trust and love for each other. If not, as in this case, if it is taken as offensive whatever the context, being a true educator has become dangerous indeed. And it would be foolish to ignore the magnification of the peril we share.

To give scandal is to shock people, to undercut their values and beliefs, to shake their very foundations. It is also problematic. If the scandal we sow issues in distrust, disbelief, hatred, despair (I think here particularly of the effect of Christopher Hitchens's and Richard Dawkins's books on naïve students), the Gospel says it would be better that a millstone be hung around our necks, and reason would tell us that we have sacrificed innocents on the altar of our own egos, to show how superior our thinking is. However, Paul speaks of another kind of scandal, precisely the kind that we have to embrace. Indeed, in an earlier interview when he was Cardinal Ratzinger, the pope referred to Paul when he said that the scandal we should focus on is the scandal of the Cross, the sacrifice entered into by the *Logos*. This scandal, which reverses the way of the world, replacing the ego at the center of our actions with *caritas*, surprising the jaded and decadent into kindness and hope, has a special home in the academia that Benedict fondly recalls. At the heart of the university there should be the sacrifice of ego, of profit, of respectability, and even of life if necessary, given up in pursuit of and witness to that reason the pope defends in his address and to truth, to knowledge, to the experiences contained within the works we explore with our students. This is indeed scandal to the contemporary world that sees the university as modeled on the assembly line of industry or the business model of pleasing customers or the computer model of fulfilling the self. Our model—Socrates' and Benedict's—requires giving up the self for the sake of something much larger, a difficult thing to teach our students and a thing that can be accomplished only by our professing. The result of such loving sacrifice undertaken daily by students and teachers is the unending and ever new discovery of a rich and various world filled with mystery, one upon which we exercise the very reason that Benedict defends in his address. It is this experience that is the fruit of the daily courage and joy, the scandal of the academic life.

Appendix

THE REGENSBURG LECTURE

Apostolic Journey of His Holiness Benedict XVI to
München, Altötting and Regensburg
(September 9–14, 2006)
Meeting with the Representatives of Science
Lecture of the Holy Father
Aula Magna of the University of Regensburg
Tuesday, 12 September 2006

Faith, Reason and the University
*Memories and Reflections**

#1) *Your Eminences, Your Magnificences, Your Excellen-cies,
Distinguished Ladies and Gentlemen,*

#2) It is a moving experience for me to be back again in the uni-versity and to be able once again to give a lecture at this podium. I think back to those years when, after a pleasant period at the Freisinger Hochschule, I began teaching at the University of Bonn. That was in 1959, in the days of the old university made up of ordi-nary professors.

#3) The various chairs had neither assistants nor secretaries, but in

recompense there was much direct contact with students and in
particular among the professors themselves. We would meet before
and after lessons in the rooms of the teaching staff. There was a
lively exchange with historians, philosophers, philologists and,
naturally, between the two theological faculties.

#4) Once a semester there was a *dies academicus*, when professors
from every faculty appeared before the students of the entire university, making possible a genuine experience of *universitas* –
something that you too, Magnificent Rector, just mentioned – the
experience, in other words, of the fact that despite our specializations which at times make it difficult to communicate with each
other, we made up a whole, working in everything on the basis of
a single rationality with its various aspects and sharing responsibility for the right use of reason – this reality became a lived experience.

#5) The university was also very proud of its two theological fac-
ulties. It was clear that, by inquiring about the reasonableness of
faith, they too carried out a work which is necessarily part of the
"whole" of the *universitas scientiarum*, even if not everyone could
share the faith which theologians seek to correlate with reason as a
whole.

#6) This profound sense of coherence within the universe of reason
was not troubled, even when it was once reported that a colleague
had said there was something odd about our university: it had two
faculties devoted to something that did not exist: God.

#7) That even in the face of such radical scepticism it is still nec-
essary and reasonable to raise the question of God through the use

of reason, and to do so in the context of the tradition of the Christian faith: this, within the university as a whole, was accepted without question.

#8) I was reminded of all this recently, when I read the edition by Professor Theodore Khoury (Münster) of part of the dialogue carried on – perhaps in 1391 in the winter barracks near Ankara – by the erudite Byzantine emperor Manuel II Paleologus and an educated Persian on the subject of Christianity and Islam, and the truth of both.[1] It was presumably the emperor himself who set down this dialogue, during the siege of Constantinople between 1394 and 1402; and this would explain why his arguments are given in greater detail than those of his Persian interlocutor.[2]

#9) The dialogue ranges widely over the structures of faith contained in the Bible and in the Qur'an, and deals especially with the image of God and of man, while necessarily returning repeatedly to the relationship between – as they were called – three "Laws" or "rules of life": the Old Testament, the New Testament and the Qur'an.

#10) It is not my intention to discuss this question in the present lecture; here I would like to discuss only one point – itself rather marginal to the dialogue as a whole – which, in the context of the issue of "faith and reason", I found interesting and which can serve as the starting-point for my reflections on this issue.

#11) In the seventh conversation (διάλεξς – controversy) edited by Professor Khoury, the emperor touches on the theme of the holy war. The emperor must have known that surah 2, 256 reads: "There is no compulsion in religion". According to some of the experts, this is probably one of the suras of the early period, when Mohammed was still powerless and under threat.

#12) But naturally the emperor also knew the instructions, developed later and recorded in the Qur'an, concerning holy war. Without descending to details, such as the difference in treatment accorded to those who have the "Book" and the "infidels", he addresses his interlocutor with a startling brusqueness, a brusqueness that we find unacceptable, on the central question about the relationship between religion and violence in general, saying: "Show me just what Mohammed brought that was new, and there you will find things only evil and inhuman, such as his command to spread by the sword the faith he preached."[3]

#13) The emperor, after having expressed himself so forcefully, goes on to explain in detail the reasons why spreading the faith through violence is something unreasonable. Violence is incompatible with the nature of God and the nature of the soul. "God", he says, "is not pleased by blood – and not acting reasonably (σὺν λόγω) is contrary to God's nature. Faith is born of the soul, not the body. Whoever would lead someone to faith needs the ability to speak well and to reason properly, without violence and threats. . . . To convince a reasonable soul, one does not need a strong arm, or weapons of any kind, or any other means of threatening a person with death. . . ."[4]

#14) The decisive statement in this argument against violent conversion is this: not to act in accordance with reason is contrary to God's nature.[5] The editor, Theodore Khoury, observes: For the emperor, as a Byzantine shaped by Greek philosophy, this statement is self-evident. But for Muslim teaching, God is absolutely transcendent. His will is not bound up with any of our categories, even that of rationality.[6]

#15) Here Khoury quotes a work of the noted French Islamist R. Arnaldez, who points out that Ibn Hazm went so far as to state that God is not bound even by his own word, and that nothing would oblige him to reveal the truth to us. Were it God's will, we would even have to practise idolatry.[7]

#16) At this point, as far as understanding of God and thus the concrete practice of religion is concerned, we are faced with an unavoidable dilemma. Is the conviction that acting unreasonably contradicts God's nature merely a Greek idea, or is it always and intrinsically true?

#17) I believe that here we can see the profound harmony between what is Greek in the best sense of the word and the Biblical understanding of faith in God. Modifying the first verse of the Book of Genesis, the first verse of the whole Bible, John began the prologue of his Gospel with the words: "In the beginning was the λόγος". This is the very word used by the emperor: God acts, σό λόγω, with *logos*. *Logos* means both reason and word – a reason which is creative and capable of self-communication, precisely as reason.

#18) John thus spoke the final word on the Biblical concept of God, and in this word all the often toilsome and tortuous threads of Biblical faith find their culmination and synthesis. In the beginning was the *logos*, and the *logos* is God, says the Evangelist.

#19) The encounter between the Biblical message and Greek thought did not happen by chance. The vision of Saint Paul, who saw the roads to Asia barred and in a dream saw a Macedonian man plead with him: "Come over to Macedonia and help us!" (cf. *Acts* 16:6–10) – this vision can be interpreted as a "distillation" of the intrinsic necessity of a rapprochement between Biblical faith and Greek inquiry.

#20) In point of fact, this rapprochement had been going on for some time. The mysterious name of God, revealed from the burning bush, a name which separates this God from all other divinities with their many names and simply asserts being, "I am", already presents a challenge to the notion of myth, to which Socrates' attempt to vanquish and transcend myth stands in close analogy.[8]

#21) Within the Old Testament, the process which started at the burning bush came to new maturity at the time of the Exile, when the God of Israel, an Israel now deprived of its land and worship, was proclaimed as the God of heaven and earth and described in a simple formula which echoes the words uttered at the burning bush: "I am". This new understanding of God is accompanied by a kind of enlightenment, which finds stark expression in the mockery of gods who are merely the work of human hands (cf. *Ps* 115).

#22) Thus, despite the bitter conflict with those Hellenistic rulers who sought to accommodate it forcibly to the customs and idolatrous cult of the Greeks, Biblical faith, in the Hellenistic period, encountered the best of Greek thought at a deep level, resulting in a mutual enrichment evident especially in the later wisdom literature.

#23) Today we know that the Greek translation of the Old Testament produced at Alexandria – the Septuagint – is more than a simple (and in that sense really less than satisfactory) translation of the Hebrew text: it is an independent textual witness and a distinct and important step in the history of revelation, one which brought about this encounter in a way that was decisive for the birth and spread of Christianity.[9]

#24) A profound encounter of faith and reason is taking place here, an encounter between genuine enlightenment and religion. From the very heart of Christian faith and, at the same time, the heart of Greek thought now joined to faith, Manuel II was able to say: Not to act "with *logos*" is contrary to God's nature.

#25) In all honesty, one must observe that in the late Middle Ages we find trends in theology which would sunder this synthesis between the Greek spirit and the Christian spirit. In contrast with the so-called intellectualism of Augustine and Thomas, there arose with Duns Scotus a voluntarism which, in its later developments, led to the claim that we can only know God's *voluntas ordinata*. Beyond this is the realm of God's freedom, in virtue of which he could have done the opposite of everything he has actually done.

#26) This gives rise to positions which clearly approach those of Ibn Hazm and might even lead to the image of a capricious God, who is not even bound to truth and goodness. God's transcendence and otherness are so exalted that our reason, our sense of the true and good, are no longer an authentic mirror of God, whose deepest possibilities remain eternally unattainable and hidden behind his actual decisions.

#27) As opposed to this, the faith of the Church has always insisted that between God and us, between his eternal Creator Spirit and our created reason there exists a real analogy, in which – as the Fourth Lateran Council in 1215 stated – unlikeness remains infinitely greater than likeness, yet not to the point of abolishing analogy and its language. God does not become more divine when we push him away from us in a sheer, impenetrable voluntarism; rather, the truly divine God is the God who has revealed himself as *logos* and, as *logos*, has acted and continues to act lovingly on our behalf. Certainly, love, as Saint Paul says, "transcends" knowledge and is thereby capable of perceiving more than thought alone (cf. *Eph* 3:19); nonetheless it continues to be love of the God who is *Logos*.

#28) Consequently, Christian worship is, again to quote Paul – "λογικη λατρεία", worship in harmony with the eternal Word and with our reason (cf. *Rom* 12:1).[10]

#29) This inner rapprochement between Biblical faith and Greek philosophical inquiry was an event of decisive importance not only from the standpoint of the history of religions, but also from that of world history – it is an event which concerns us even today. Given this convergence, it is not surprising that Christianity, despite its origins and some significant developments in the East, finally took on its historically decisive character in Europe.

#30) We can also express this the other way around: this convergence, with the subsequent addition of the Roman heritage, created Europe and remains the foundation of what can rightly be called Europe.

#31) The thesis that the critically purified Greek heritage forms an integral part of Christian faith has been countered by the call for a dehellenization of Christianity – a call which has more and more dominated theological discussions since the beginning of the modern age. Viewed more closely, three stages can be observed in the programme of dehellenization: although interconnected, they are clearly distinct from one another in their motivations and objectives.[11]

#32) Dehellenization first emerges in connection with the postulates of the Reformation in the sixteenth century.

#33) Looking at the tradition of scholastic theology, the Reformers thought they were confronted with a faith system totally conditioned by philosophy, that is to say an articulation of the faith based on an alien system of thought. As a result, faith no longer appeared as a living historical Word but as one element of an overarching philosophical system.

#34) The principle of *sola scriptura*, on the other hand, sought faith in its pure, primordial form, as originally found in the Biblical Word. Metaphysics appeared as a premise derived from another source, from which faith had to be liberated in order to become once more fully itself.

#35) When Kant stated that he needed to set thinking aside in order to make room for faith, he carried this programme forward with a radicalism that the Reformers could never have foreseen. He thus anchored faith exclusively in practical reason, denying it access to reality as a whole.

#36) The liberal theology of the nineteenth and twentieth centuries ushered in a second stage in the process of dehellenization, with Adolf von Harnack as its outstanding representative.

#37) When I was a student, and in the early years of my teaching, this programme was highly influential in Catholic theology too. It took as its point of departure Pascal's distinction between the God of the philosophers and the God of Abraham, Isaac and Jacob. In my inaugural lecture at Bonn in 1959, I tried to address the issue,[12] and I do not intend to repeat here what I said on that occasion, but I would like to describe at least briefly what was new about this second stage of dehellenization.

#38) Harnack's central idea was to return simply to the man Jesus and to his simple message, underneath the accretions of theology and indeed of hellenization: this simple message was seen as the culmination of the religious development of humanity. Jesus was said to have put an end to worship in favour of morality. In the end he was presented as the father of a humanitarian moral message.

#39) Fundamentally, Harnack's goal was to bring Christianity back into harmony with modern reason, liberating it, that is to say, from seemingly philosophical and theological elements, such as faith in Christ's divinity and the triune God. In this sense, historical-critical exegesis of the New Testament, as he saw it, restored to theology its place within the university: theology, for Harnack, is something essentially historical and therefore strictly scientific. What it is able to say critically about Jesus is, so to speak, an expression of practical reason and consequently it can take its rightful place within the university.

#40) Behind this thinking lies the modern self-limitation of reason, classically expressed in Kant's "Critiques", but in the meantime further radicalized by the impact of the natural sciences. This modern concept of reason is based, to put it briefly, on a synthesis between Platonism (Cartesianism) and empiricism, a synthesis confirmed by the success of technology.

#41) On the one hand it presupposes the mathematical structure of matter, its intrinsic rationality, which makes it possible to understand how matter works and use it efficiently: this basic premise is, so to speak, the Platonic element in the modern understanding of nature.

#42) On the other hand, there is nature's capacity to be exploited for our purposes, and here only the possibility of verification or falsification through experimentation can yield decisive certainty.

#43) The weight between the two poles can, depending on the circumstances, shift from one side to the other. As strongly positivistic a thinker as J. Monod has declared himself a convinced Platonist/Cartesian.

#44) This gives rise to two principles which are crucial for the issue we have raised.

#45) First, only the kind of certainty resulting from the interplay of mathematical and empirical elements can be considered scientific. Anything that would claim to be science must be measured against this criterion. Hence the human sciences, such as history, psychology, sociology and philosophy, attempt to conform themselves to this canon of scientificity.

#46) A second point, which is important for our reflections, is that by its very nature this method excludes the question of God, making it appear an unscientific or pre-scientific question.

Consequently, we are faced with a reduction of the radius of science and reason, one which needs to be questioned.

#47) I will return to this problem later. In the meantime, it must be observed that from this standpoint any attempt to maintain theology's claim to be "scientific" would end up reducing Christianity to a mere fragment of its former self.

#48) But we must say more: if science as a whole is this and this alone, then it is man himself who ends up being reduced, for the specifically human questions about our origin and destiny, the questions raised by religion and ethics, then have no place within the purview of collective reason as defined by "science", so understood, and must thus be relegated to the realm of the subjective. The subject then decides, on the basis of his experiences, what he considers tenable in matters of religion, and the subjective "conscience" becomes the sole arbiter of what is ethical.

#49) In this way, though, ethics and religion lose their power to create a community and become a completely personal matter. This is a dangerous state of affairs for humanity, as we see from the disturbing pathologies of religion and reason which necessarily erupt when reason is so reduced that questions of religion and ethics no longer concern it. Attempts to construct an ethic from the rules of evolution or from psychology and sociology, end up being simply inadequate.

#50) Before I draw the conclusions to which all this has been leading, I must briefly refer to the third stage of dehellenization, which is now in progress.

#51) In the light of our experience with cultural pluralism, it is often said nowadays that the synthesis with Hellenism achieved in the early Church was an initial inculturation which ought not to be binding on other cultures. The latter are said to have the right to return to the simple message of the New Testament prior to that inculturation, in order to inculturate it anew in their own particular milieux.

#52) This thesis is not simply false, but it is coarse and lacking in precision. The New Testament was written in Greek and bears the imprint of the Greek spirit, which had already come to maturity as the Old Testament developed.

#53) True, there are elements in the evolution of the early Church which do not have to be integrated into all cultures. Nonetheless, the fundamental decisions made about the relationship between faith and the use of human reason are part of the faith itself; they are developments consonant with the nature of faith itself.

#54) And so I come to my conclusion. This attempt, painted with broad strokes, at a critique of modern reason from within has nothing to do with putting the clock back to the time before the Enlightenment and rejecting the insights of the modern age. The positive aspects of modernity are to be acknowledged unreservedly: we are all grateful for the marvellous possibilities that it has opened up for mankind and for the progress in humanity that has been granted to us.

#55) The scientific ethos, moreover, is – as you yourself mentioned, Magnificent Rector – the will to be obedient to the truth, and, as such, it embodies an attitude which belongs to the essential decisions of the Christian spirit.

#56) The intention here is not one of retrenchment or negative criticism, but of broadening our concept of reason and its application. While we rejoice in the new possibilities open to humanity, we also see the dangers arising from these possibilities and we must ask ourselves how we can overcome them. We will succeed in doing so only if reason and faith come together in a new way, if we overcome the self-imposed limitation of reason to the empirically falsifiable, and if we once more disclose its vast horizons.

#57) In this sense theology rightly belongs in the university and within the wide-ranging dialogue of sciences, not merely as a historical discipline and one of the human sciences, but precisely as theology, as inquiry into the rationality of faith. Only thus do we become capable of that genuine dialogue of cultures and religions so urgently needed today.

#58) In the Western world it is widely held that only positivistic reason and the forms of philosophy based on it are universally valid. Yet the world's profoundly religious cultures see this exclusion of the divine from the universality of reason as an attack on their most profound convictions. A reason which is deaf to the divine and which relegates religion into the realm of subcultures is incapable of entering into the dialogue of cultures.

#59) At the same time, as I have attempted to show, modern scientific reason with its intrinsically Platonic element bears within itself a question which points beyond itself and beyond the possibilities of its methodology. Modern scientific reason quite simply has to accept the rational structure of matter and the correspondence between our spirit and the prevailing rational structures of nature as a given, on which its methodology has to be based.

#60) Yet the question why this has to be so is a real question, and one which has to be remanded by the natural sciences to other modes and planes of thought – to philosophy and theology. For philosophy and, albeit in a different way, for theology, listening to the great experiences and insights of the religious traditions of humanity, and those of the Christian faith in particular, is a source of knowledge, and to ignore it would be an unacceptable restriction of our listening and responding.

#61) Here I am reminded of something Socrates said to Phaedo. In their earlier conversations, many false philosophical opinions had been raised, and so Socrates says: "It would be easily understandable if someone became so annoyed at all these false notions that for the rest of his life he despised and mocked all talk about being – but in this way he would be deprived of the truth of existence and would suffer a great loss".[13]

#62) The West has long been endangered by this aversion to the questions which underlie its rationality, and can only suffer great harm thereby. The courage to engage the whole breadth of reason, and not the denial of its grandeur – this is the programme with which a theology grounded in Biblical faith enters into the debates of our time.

#63) "Not to act reasonably, not to act with *logos*, is contrary to the nature of God", said Manuel II, according to his Christian understanding of God, in response to his Persian interlocutor. It is to this great *logos*, to this breadth of reason, that we invite our partners in the dialogue of cultures. To rediscover it constantly is the great task of the university.

Endnotes

*   Copyright 2006 – Libreria Editrice Vaticana.

1.   Of the total number of 26 conversations (διά λεξις – Khoury translates this as "controversy") in the dialogue ("Entretien"), T. Khoury published the 7th "controversy" with footnotes and an extensive introduction on the origin of the text, on the manuscript tradition and on the structure of the dialogue, together with brief summaries of the "controversies" not included in the edition; the Greek text is accompanied by a French translation: "Manuel II Paléologue, Entretiens avec un Musulman. 7ᵉ Controverse", *Sources Chrétiennes* n. 115, Paris 1966. In the meantime, Karl Förstel published in *Corpus Islamico-Christianum (Series Graeca* ed. A. T. Khoury and R. Glei) an edition of the text in Greek and German with commentary: "Manuel II. Palaiologus, Dialoge mit einem Muslim", 3 vols., Würzburg-Altenberge 1993–1996. As early as 1966, E. Trapp had published the Greek text with an introduction as vol. II of *Wiener byzantinische Studien*. I shall be quoting from Khoury's edition.

2.   On the origin and redaction of the dialogue, cf. Khoury, pp. 22–29; extensive comments in this regard can also be found in the editions of Förstel and Trapp.

3.   Controversy VII, 2 c: Khoury, pp. 142–143;• Förstel, vol. I, VII. Dialog 1.5, pp. 240–241. In the Muslim world, this quotation has unfortunately been taken as an expression of my personal position, thus arousing understandable indignation.• I hope that the reader of my text can see immediately that this sentence does not express my personal view of the Qur'an, for which I have the respect due to the holy book of a great religion.• In quoting the text of the Emperor Manuel II, I intended solely to draw out the essential relationship between faith and reason.•On this point I am in agreement with Manuel II, but without endorsing his polemic.

4.   Controversy VII, 3 b–c: Khoury, pp. 144–145; Förstel vol. I, VII. Dialog 1.6, pp. 240–243.

5.   It was purely for the sake of this statement that I quoted the dialogue between Manuel and his Persian interlocutor. In this statement the theme of my subsequent reflections emerges.

6. Cf. Khoury, p. 144, n. 1.
7. R. Arnaldez, *Grammaire et théologie chez Ibn Hazm de Cordoue*, Paris 1956, p. 13; cf. Khoury, p. 144. The fact that comparable positions exist in the theology of the late Middle Ages will appear later in my discourse.
8. Regarding the widely discussed interpretation of the episode of the burning bush, I refer to my book *Introduction to Christianity,* London 1969, pp. 77–93 (originally published in German as *Einführung in das Christentum,* Munich 1968; N.B. the pages quoted refer to the entire chapter entitled "The Biblical Belief in God"). I think that my statements in that book, despite later developments in the discussion, remain valid today.
9. Cf. A. Schenker, "L'Écriture sainte subsiste en plusieurs formes canoniques simultanées", in *L'Interpretazione della Bibbia nella Chiesa. Atti del Simposio promosso dalla Congregazione per la Dottrina della Fede*, Vatican City 2001, pp. 178–186.
10. On this matter I expressed myself in greater detail in my book *The Spirit of the Liturgy*, San Francisco 2000, pp. 44–50.
11. Of the vast literature on the theme of dehellenization, I would like to mention above all: A. Grillmeier, "Hellenisierung-Judaisierung des Christentums als Deuteprinzipien der Geschichte des kirchlichen Dogmas", in idem, *Mit ihm und in ihm. Christologische Forschungen und Perspektiven*, Freiburg 1975, pp. 423–488.
12. Newly published with commentary by Heino Sonnemans (ed.): *Joseph Ratzinger-Benedikt XVI, Der Gott des Glaubens und der Gott der Philosophen. Ein Beitrag zum Problem der theologia naturalis*, Johannes-Verlag Leutesdorf, 2nd revised edition, 2005.
13. Cf. 90 c–d. For this text, cf. also R. Guardini, *Der Tod des Sokrates*, 5th edition, Mainz-Paderborn 1987, pp. 218–221.

Contributors

GLENN ARBERY is the author of *Why Literature Matters: Permanence and the Politics of Reputation*, editor of *The Tragic Abyss*, and author of essays on Homer, Dante, Shakespeare, Dostoevsky, modern poetry, and Southern literature. He is currently D'Alzon Visiting Professor at Assumption College.

BAINARD COWAN is author of *Exiled Waters:* Moby-Dick *and the Crisis of Allegory* and editor of three books of essays on American literature, literature of the Americas, and liberal education. He holds the Cowan Chair in Literature at the University of Dallas.

JEAN BETHKE ELSHTAIN is Laura Spelman Rockefeller Professor of Social and Political Ethics in the University of Chicago Divinity School. She is a contributing editor for *The New Republic* and author of over five hundred essays and over a dozen books, including *Sovereignty: God, State, and Self*, based on the prestigious Gifford Lectures which she recently gave at the University of Edinburgh.

After completing coursework for a Ph.D. in political philosophy at Notre Dame, BRUCE FINGERHUT went into book publishing, first at Open Court, then at Notre Dame Press, before becoming a founder of Gateway Editions (now Regnery). Later he founded a trade press, a spoken-audio distributor, and a scholarly catalogue dealing with books in philosophy. In 1996, he founded St. Augustine's Press, which has become a leading scholarly publisher in philosophy, theology, and cultural history.

MARC D. GUERRA is the author of *Christians as Political Animals: Taking the Measure of Modernity and Modern Democracy.*

PETER AUGUSTINE LAWLER is Dana Professor of Government and International Studies at Berry College, executive editor of the journal *Perspectives on Political Science*, and author or editor of a dozen books, including *Stuck with Virtue: The American Individual and Our Biotechnological Future*, and *Homeless and at Home in America.* He is the recipient of the 2007 Richard M. Weaver Prize for Scholarly Letters.

MICHAEL MCSHANE is associate professor in Great Ideas and Philosophy at Carthage College. He is working on a book about Shakespeare's *King Lear.*

MARY MUMBACH is a founder of the Thomas More College of Liberal Arts and of the Erasmus Institute of Liberal Arts, where she is dean of the college and professor of literature. She has published essays on medieval romance, on Shakespeare, on Faulkner, on Flannery O'Connor, and on education.

NALIN RANASINGHE is an associate professor of philosophy at Assumption College. He is the author of *The Soul of Socrates* and *Socrates in the Underworld* and the editor of *Eros and Logos.* Currently completing the third volume of his Socratic trilogy,

Socrates and the Gods, he has also published essays and reviews on subjects ranging from Homer and the Book of Job to Shakespeare, Kant, Nietzsche, and Hannah Arendt.

R. R. RENO is Professor of Theology at Creighton University and an editor at *First Things*. He is the author or co-author of five books, including *In the Ruins of the Church: Sustaining Faith in an Age of Diminished Christianity*, and is General Editor of the 40-volume *Brazos Theological Commentary on the Bible*, which includes his commentary on Genesis.